The Rural Elderly

The Rural Elderly
An Annotated Bibliography of Social Science Research

COMPILED BY JOHN A. KROUT

Greenwood Press
Westport, Connecticut • London, England

Library of Congress Cataloging in Publication Data

Krout, John A.
    The rural elderly.

    Bibliography: p.
    Includes indexes.
    1. Rural aged—United States—Bibliography.
I. Title.
Z7164.04K76   1983   016.3052'6'0973   83-10881
[HQ1064.U5]
ISBN 0-313-23509-0 (lib. bdg.)

Library of Congress Catalog Card Number: 83-10881
ISBN: 0-313-23509-0

First published in 1983

Greenwood Press
A division of Congressional Information Service, Inc.
88 Post Road West, Westport, Connecticut 06881

Printed in the United States of America

10 9 8 7 6 5 4 3 2 1

To
My Parents

CONTENTS

Contents

PREFACE

This bibliography attempts to provide a comprehensive review of existing social science research on America's rural elderly. It is true that there is far less research available on the rural than the urban elderly. However, the works annotated here attest to the growing and diverse interest among researchers and practitioners in the elderly who live outside of larger urban areas. After searching for literature on the rural elderly for over two years, the author has been impressed by the multitude of sources where such work can be found. While much more research certainly needs to be done in this area, the existing knowledge should be assessed, organized, and integrated before new works are undertaken. It is hoped that this bibliography will at least provide some of the organization so that other efforts can be directed towards the assessment and integration.

The term "rural" is used here not to refer to a specific type of place but a wide range of places that by common understanding are seen as different from big cities and the sprawling suburban areas that spread from them. Thus, works on areas variously described as farm, rural nonfarm, village, small town, and nonmetropolitan are included in this bibliography. Since the debate on exactly what "rural" is has gone on for a long time and still continues, any decision to attach an overly restrictive meaning to the term would be presumptuous. It seems to the author that the term should and must be viewed as representing a continuum of living environments.

Therefore, in compiling this bibliography a wide range of key works indicating rural were looked for. General works on the aged were not included nor were works that only considered residence as a minor variable in a larger study. To be eligible for inclusion, a work had to examine questions directly relevant to and for the elderly who lived in rural/nonmetroplitan type areas or on rural/nonrural comparisons, and to be carried out on America's rural elderly. These restrictions were put in place to reduce the bibliography to a manageable size and to provide a clear focus for the work. In addition, while this bibliography primarily covers social science research, works on planning, policy, and programs (so-called "applied" areas) are also included.

The chronological coverage of material presented in this bibliography is not restricted. Not surprisingly, only a few of the citations predate 1970 (11 percent). Some 24 percent of the works noted here appeared between 1970-1975, 47 percent between 1976-1980, and 18 percent are post-1980.

A large number of potential sources of information on the rural elderly were examined during the compilation of this work. Computer searches of major document files were carried out, general bibliographies were reviewed, professional meeting programs were scrutinized, and countless reference lists from articles on the rural elderly were explored. The result of this effort is the 590 individual citations found in this bibliography referring to journal articles, books, book chapters, government reports and hearings, theses, dissertations, grant reports, conference proceedings, conference paper presentations, bibliographies, experiment station publications, and unpublished manuscripts.

Each citation provides information on the author, title, date, and place of publication. In addition, the vast majority of these citations are annotated and include, where appropriate, a brief description of where the study was conducted, sample size, research problems, and major findings. Works that cover a large number of topics or are more argumentative than descriptive or analytical are annotated differently. Here the coverage of the work on the author's main points are noted. A small number of works are simply referenced and not annotated.

The organization of the bibliography is straightforward. Each of the references is placed alphabetically by the author's last name in one of the twenty-nine subject headings (also listed alphabetically).

The citations are also cross-referenced in additional subject areas (first author only). This cross-referencing is done in cases where a work investigates several phenomena or the relationship between them, and will hopefully allow the reader to zero in on his or her area of interest with greater ease and accuracy. There are a total of 284 cross-references in this bibliography. Two indexes are provided at the end of this work: an author index that lists the entry numbers of first authors only and does not include cross-references, and a geographic index that lists entry numbers by state, region, or area.

In sum, this annotated bibliography has been compiled to provide a comprehensive listing (through 1982) and description of both pure and applied research in the area of the rural elderly. It is highly likely that some relevant publications and papers on this topic have been inadvertently excluded from this work. Such was not the intent, and it is hoped that the affected parties understand this to be so.

It would appear that the rich variety of contexts in which rural aging research is performed is both a boon and a curse. While there is a large body of literature to learn from, it is sometimes difficult to identify all of this work because of the large number of forums in which it is presented. This bibliography is intended to serve as an up-to-date reference work for researchers, practitioners, and policy planners and hopefully will assist them in their present and future work on or with the rural elderly.

John A. Krout
Fredonia, New York

ACKNOWLEDGMENTS

No work can be credited to solely one person and this bibliography is no exception. Many people contributed to the completion of this project and all of them deserve recognition. The staff of the Reed Library at the State University of New York, College at Fredonia processed countless interlibrary loan requests, provided expert reference advice, and assisted in computer searches of various files. Several staff members of Greenwood Press encouraged, guided, and assisted me with this project for over a year; Paul Kobasa and Margaret Brezicki, in particular.

Special thanks and recognition go to two individuals without whom this bibliography would never have been completed. Vivian Larson provided invaluable assistance and a lot of hard work in almost every aspect of this project. Barbara Nobbs Krout contributed her expert typing, proofing, and organizational skills, not to mention accepting an endless number of excuses from a spouse who was "working on the Bib."

Credit must also be given to all those colleagues whose works are referenced herein. In many ways, this bibliography is as much theirs as it is mine. Of course, as is customary in most works such as this, the author takes full responsibility for mistakes, oversights, or omissions found in this work.

The Rural Elderly

BIBLIOGRAPHY

ATTITUDES AND VALUES

1. Bley, N., D. Dye, K. Jensen, and M. Goodman. "Client's Perceptions - Key Variable in Evaluating Activities for the Elderly." The Gerontologist, 12:(1972).

    Describes an evaluation process aimed at determining the attitudes of the elderly towards recreational services. The authors argue that the rural elderly in particular should be allowed the opportunity to express their leisure activity needs.

2. Crase, Darrell. "Southern Appalachia and the Health Behavior of the Aging." Lifelong Learning: The Adult Years, 1:4-7 (January, 1978).

    A description of health attitudes and behavior of southern Appalachians. Discusses the impact of institutionalized care and supporting agencies.

3. Foerster, Lloyd (ed.), The Aging in Rural Mid-America: A Symposium on Values for an Evolving Quality of Life, June 5-6, 1978. Lindsberg, Kansas: Bethany College Publications, June 5-6, 1978.

    Seven addresses given at the Work Conference on Aging held at Bethany College. Focusing on rural aging, the goal of the conference was to stimulate ideas useful to participants.

4. Kim, Paul K. H. See entry number 152.

5. Landis, Judson T. "Attitudes and adjustments of aged rural people in Iowa." (Doctoral dissertation, Louisiana State University, 1940.) Dissertation Abstracts International, W1940, p.99.

6. Levy, Jerrold E. See entry number 421.

7. McMillen, Marilyn. See entry number 214.

8. Myska, M. J., and R. A. Pasewark. "Death Attitudes of Residential and Non-residential Rural Aged Persons." Psychological Reports, 43(3):1235-1238 (1978).

    Reports on the attitudes toward death among ambulatory patients of a Wyoming state multi-purpose institution for the elderly.

9. Pihlblad, C. Terence. "Culture, Life-style, and Social Environments of the Small Town." In Robert C. Atchley with Thomas O. Byerts (eds.), Rural Environments and Aging. Washington, D. C.: Gerontological Society, 1975. Pp. 47-62.

    This paper is based on studies of elderly residents of small towns in Missouri. Addresses the following topics: values and social climate of the small town, the status system, and the role of the elderly.

10. Powers, Edward A., and Gordon L. Bultena. "Correspondence Between Anticipated and Actual Uses of Public Services by the Aged." Social Service Review, 48:245-254 (1974).

    Using longitudinal data, the authors document a lack of conqruity between attitudes toward services and subsequent use of those services by the elderly living in five nonmetropolitan Iowa counties. The authors conclude that needs were met by other sources than public programs are not seen as explanations of nonuse. Nonuse is seen as associated with a desire to avoid a definition of self as old and the appearance of receiving charity.

11. Sebastian, Margaret, and Eileen Payne. "Health Care for Rural Older Women: Attitudes Toward Nurse Practitioners." In Paul K. H. Kim and C. P. Wilson (eds.), Toward Mental Health of the Rural Elderly. Washington, D. C.: University Press of America, 1981. Pp. 195-203.

    Explores the feasability of nurse practitioners providing health care to elderly rural women. In 1978 115 women aged 55 to 91 completed questionnaires assessing their health, barriers to health care, and attitudes toward nurse practitioners. The survey was conducted in southeastern Ohio. Findings indicate an acceptance of the nurse practitioners concept.

12. Wass, Hannelore. See entry number 30.

13. White, Melvin A., Rocky Mountain Gerontology Center, Salt Lake City, Utah. "The Values of the Rural Aged." Paper presented at the Western Gerontological Association Meeting (Denver, Colorado; March, 1977).

14.   White, Melvin A.   "Values of Elderly Differ in Rural
Setting."   Generations, 2(3):6-7 (Fall, 1977).

      This short article identifies and describes the value
      orientations of the rural elderly.   Those values dis-
      cussed are: independence, hard work, freedom, sense
      of accomplishment, conservatism, integrity, and respon-
      sibility.   The author also discusses the implications
      of the rural elderly's values on social service and
      health programs.

15.   Youmans, E. Grant.   See entry number 800.

16.   Youmans, E. Grant.   See entry number 802.

17.   Youmans, E. Grant.   See entry number 805.

CHURCH AND RELIGION

18.   Collier, Charlotte Meier.   "A community study of aging
and religion among rural Pennsylvania Germans."   (Doctoral
dissertation, Cultural Anthropology, University of Massachusetts, 1978.)   Dissertation Abstracts International, 39, 8,
A, p.5012.

      A study of the relationship between religion and com-
      munity integration.   Data are from 164 elderly resi-
      dents of a small town in rural southeastern Pennsylva-
      nia.   Religion was found to be an important part of
      their lives.

19.   Davis, Katherine Conway.   "The Position and Status of
Black and White Aged in Rural Baptist Churches in Missouri."
The Journal of Minority Aging, 5(3):242-248 (1980).

      Examines the status held by the elderly in three rural
      Missouri churches (one white and two black).   The elder-
      ly are found to have high status in all churches.

20.   Karcher, Charles J.   See entry number 566.

21.   Stevenson, John Robert.   "The development of a lay min-
istry to elderly and shut-in members of the rural Valley
United Presbyterian Church."   (Doctoral dissertation, Drew
University, Madison, New Jersey, 1980.)   Dissertation Abstracts International, 41, 5, A, p.2161.

      Disscusses the development of a lay ministry to rural
      elderly church members who were unable to participate
      in community and/or church activities due to age or
      illness.   Not a social science study per sey.

22.   Tellis-Nayak V.   "The Puritan religious ethos of the
rural elderly: The functionalist pitfall."   Oneonta, New
York: Hartwick College, 1981.

23. Wilkinson, Carroll Wetzel. See entry number 179.

CRIME

24. Clemente, Frank, and Michael B. Kleiman. "Fear of Crime Among the Aged." The Gerontologist, 16:207-210 (1976).

> This study uses national data to examine patterns of fear of crime among the aged and non-aged. The data are examined using four key variables - sex, race, socioeconomic status, and size of community. The elderly express greater fear of crime than the non-elderly as do nonblacks and those with lower incomes. Fear of crime was also found to be positively associated with community size. Elderly living in large cities were three times as likely as rural elderly to express a fear of crime.

25. Donnermeyer, Joseph F., G. Howard Phillips, and Mary Jo Steiner. "Age, Fear of Crime, and Victimization in Rural Areas." Paper presented at the Annual Meeting of the North Central Sociological Association (1981).

26. Lee, Gary R. See entry number 755.

27. Liley, Floyd Wilbur. "The development of a burglary prevention training module for elderly persons living in a rural area." (Doctoral dissertation, University of Southern Mississippi, February, 1982.) Dissertation Abstracts International, 42, 8, A, p.3387.

> This study describes the development, planning, and evaluation of a burglary prevention training module for the aged living in a rural community. The training module consisted of a slide presentation, exercise and evaluation instruments, and informational materials. The module increased the elderly's knowledge of burglarly prevention techniques and was favorably received by them.

DEATH AND DYING

28. Murphey, Millede. See entry number 765.

29. Myska, M. J. See entry number 8.

30. Wass, Hannelore. "Views and Opinions of Elderly Persons Concerning Death." Educational Gerontology, 2(1):15-26 (January-March, 1977).

> Examines data on the elderly's views and opinions concerning death and dying from three groups of elderly (one of them rural).

31. Wilkinson, Carroll Wetzel. See entry number 178.

32. Wilkinson, Carroll Wetzel. See entry number 179.

DEMOGRAPHICS

33. Aizenberg, Rhonda, and Maurice D. Van Arsdol, Jr. "Metropolitan/Nonmetropolitan Movements Among the Aged." Paper presented at the Annual Meeting of the Gerontological Society of America (San Diego, California; November, 1980).

> Examines the residential mobility of the elderly from a metro/nonmetro focus. Compares characteristics of older movers and nonmovers and assess the relative influence of a number of factors on metro/nonmetro movement among the elderly. Uses data from the 1978 Census Current Population Studies.

34. Beal, C. L. Composition of Farm and Rural Populations. Washington, D. C.: United States Department of Agriculture, 1976.

> A report examining the socio-demographic composition of the rural population. Presents data on the number of aged on farms.

35. Clifford, William B. See entry number 730.

36. Fuguitt, Glen V., and Stephen J. Tordella. "Elderly Net Migration: The New Trend of Nonmetropolitan Population Change." Research on Aging, 2:191-204 (June, 1980).

> Examines changes in the pattern of elderly net migration for nonmetropolitan and metropolitan areas between 1950 and 1975. Elderly nonmetropolitan net migration rates were positive for both the 1960's and 1970's and larger than those for metropolitan areas. The authors analyzed net migration data for 3,100 U.S. counties or county equivalents.

37. Gillaspy, R. T. "Migration of the Older Population to Low Income Counties." Paper presented at the Annual Meeting of the Gerontological Society of America (Dallas, Texas; November, 1978).

38. Hanreider, B. D. "Where the Elderly Live. Methods for Intercensal Estimates of the Elderly Population in the U.S. in Small Geographic Areas." The Gerontologist, 17(5): (October, 1977).

> A brief discussion of two techniques to estimate the size of the small town elderly population between censuses.

39. Heaton, Tim B., William B. Clifford, and Glenn V. Fuguitt. "Changing Patterns of Retirement Migration: Movement

Between Metropolitan and Nonmetropolitan Areas." Research on Aging, 2:93-104 (March, 1980).

> Relying on 1960 and 1970 census data and the March, 1975 Current Population Survey the authors compare migration between metropolitan and nonmetropolitan areas. Three time periods are examined: 1955-1960, 1965-1970, and 1970-1975.

40. Kim, Paul K. H. See entry number 151.

41. Kivett, Vira R., and R. Max Learner. "Perspectives on the Childless Rural Elderly: A Comparative Analysis." The Gerontologist, 20:708-710 (December, 1980).

> Includes a thorough review of literature on the parent-child relationship of older adults and a secondary analysis of a data base of 418 older rural adults from North Carolina. Results show few consequences of childlessness. Authors stress need to strengthen informal helping networks for all elderly.

42. Koebernick, Thomas E., and J. Allen Beegle. "Migration of the elderly to rural areas: A Case Study in Michigan." In Patterns of Migration and Population Change in America's Heartland. Research Report #344. East Lansing, Michigan: Michigan State University, Agricultural Experiment Station, 1978.

> An examination of 156 elderly households who migrated into a rural Michigan community. The authors present data on the decision to migrate and on the elderly's adjustment to relocation.

43. Krout, John A. "Seasonal Migration of the Elderly." Paper presented at the Annual Meeting of the Population Association of America (San Diego, California; April, 1982). Forthcoming in The Gerontologist.

> Examines data on the seasonal migration of a sample of some 1,300 age 60 and over residents of a New York nonmetropolitan county. Seasonal migrants were more likely to own a car and/or home, less likely to be working, and reported higher levels of income than non-migrants. Fully 4/5 chose a destination in the southeast and selected "better climate" as their first choice reason for seasonal migration.

44. Kwan, Y. H. See entry number 751.

45. Kwan, Y. H. See entry number 752.

46. Longino, Charles F. "Residential Relocation of Older People - Metro and Nonmetro." Research on Aging, 2(2):205-216 (June, 1980).

This article examines the metropolitan/nonmetropolitan migration between 1965 and 1970 of the aged 60 and over. Data are from the 1970 Public Use Sample tapes. More than half of the elderly migrants moved within or between metropolitan settings. Of those who changed their residential environment, more moved to nonmetro than metro areas. The characteristics of migrants are also discussed.

47. Longino, Charles F. "Changing Aged Nonmetropolitan Migration Patterns, 1955-60 and 1965-70." Journal of Gerontology, 37(2):228-234 (March, 1982).

This article examines elderly migration patterns between metropolitan and nonmetropolitan areas between 1960 and 1970. Rather than focus on net migration rates, the author uses data from the 1-in-100 public use samples compiled by the census. The data indicate decreased migration into metropolitan from nonmetropolitan areas leading to an overall elderly "migration turnaround" in favor of smaller places.

48. Marshall, Douglas G. "Migration and Older People in a Rural Community: The Story of Price County, Wisconsin." In Arnold M. Rose and Warren A. Peterson (eds.), Older People and Their Social World. Philadelphia, Pennsylvania: F. A. Davis Co., 1965. Pp. 341-355.

Presents a history and explanation of migration in this rural county. Special attention to the effects on the elderly and to what the future may bring.

49. Myllymaki, Judy. See entry number 463.

50. Sheldon, Henry D. "Distribution of the Rural Aged Population." In E. Grant Youmans (ed.), Older Rural Americans. Lexington, Kentucky: University of Kentucky Press, 1967. Pp. 117-143.

Discusses trends in the age structure of the United States and of the rural population focusing on the aged 65 and over population. Based largely on 1960 census data.

51. Taietz, Philip. "Community Structure and Aging." Paper presented at the 7th International Congress of Gerontology (Veinna/Austria; June 26-July 2, 1966).

Describes and analyzes the influence of community structure on the adjustment of the aged and their integration into the community. Data are from 90 New York State communities with populations from 1,000 to 100,000.

52. Tucker, Charles Jackson. "Changes in Age Composition of the Rural Black Population of the South 1950 to 1970.

Phylon, 35:268-275 (September, 1974).

   Discussion and explanation of changes in the rural black
   population of the south 1950 to 1970. Notes the 20th
   century decline of the rural black population in the
   south due to out migration has been almost totally in
   the farm segment and has changed the regions age structure. Between 1950 and 1970 the median age of the farm
   population has increased.

53. United States Bureau of the Census. Census of Population: 1970 Metropolitan and Nonmetropolitan Residence of
the Population 65 Years Old and Over: 1970. Washington, D.
C.: Bureau of the Census, 1972 (April).

54. United States Bureau of the Census. "Demographic Aspects
of Aging and the Older Population in the United States."
Current Population Reports Series P-23, No. 59. Washington,
D. C.: United States Bureau of the Census, 1976.

   Presents data on the demographic characteristics of
   the elderly population broken down by urban and rural
   residence.

55. Wang, Ching-Li. "Elderly migration, retirement function
and community growth in nonmetropolitan areas." (Doctoral
dissertation, Michigan State University, East Lansing, Michigan, July, 1977.) Dissertation Abstracts International, 39,
1, A, p.495.

   An investigation of correlates of elderly migration to
   nonmetropolitan areas, its impacts on these areas, and
   the development of retirement functions in such places.
   The author examines census data for the 1960 and 1975
   period and focuses on the North Central region. The
   amenities of nonmetropolitan areas are found to be major
   determinants of elderly in-migration.

56. Wang, Ching-Li, and J. Allen Beegle. "Impact of Elderly
Migration on the Revival of Population Growth in Nonmetropolitan Areas of the North Central Region." Paper presented
at the Annual Meeting of the Rural Sociological Society
(Madison, Wisconsin; 1977).

57. Wang, Ching-Li, and J. Allen Beegle. "Retirement func-
tion and community growth in Michigan nonmetro areas." East
Lansing, Michigan: Michigan Department of Management and
Budget and Michigan State University, 1978.

58. Wang, Ching-Li, and J. Allen Beegle. "Migration of Older People to Nonmetropolitan Areas in the North Central Region of the United States." Paper presented at the Annual
Meeting of the Rural Sociological Society (Burlington, Vermont; August, 1979).

Investigates the impact of community characteristics on elderly net migration between 1960-1970 for over 900 nonmetropolitan counties. Past migration is found to be the strongest correlate of elderly migration.

59. Wilkinson, Carroll Wetzel. See entry number 178.

60. Wilkinson, Carroll Wetzel. See entry number 179.

DRINKING AND DRUGS

61. Bainton, Barry. "Drinking Patterns of the Rural Aged." In C. L. Fry (ed.), Dimensions: Aging, Culture, and Health. New York, New York: J. F. Bergin Publishers, 1981.

62. Ballantine, John R., and Paul K. H. Kim. "Rural Elderly and Drug Use." Paper presented at the Annual Meeting of the Gerontological Society of America (Washington, D. C.; 1979).

63. Christopherson, Victor A. "Alcohol Use Among the Rural Elderly in Arizona." Paper presented at a conference on Research and Public Service with the Rural Elderly at the Western Rural Development Center, Oregon State University (Corvallis, Oregon; October, 1980). Pp. 65-75.

A study of alcohol usage among Arizona's rural elderly. Data was collected via interviews and questionnaires and detailed information was collected on the how much, how often, when, where, and why of elderly alcohol consumption. Includes a detailed account of drinking behavior among Mexican-Americans.

64. Escher, M. C. "Alcohol Usage and Health Among the Rural Elderly." Paper presented at the Annual Meeting of the Rural Sociological Society (Burlington, Vermont; August, 1979).

Examines the role of alcohol consumption in the lives of the rural elderly. Questionnaires were administered to 470 persons 65 and older living in Arizona's 12 rural counties. Discusses the relationship between health and drinking behavior.

65. Kim, Paul K. H., E. Hall, J. Augsburger, and John Ballantine. "Rural Elderly and Drug Uses." Paper presented at the 32nd Annual Meeting of the Gerontological Society of America (Washington, D. C.; November, 1979).

Determines the drug-use habits of rural older persons in central and eastern Kentucky through personal interviews with 150 elderly. Offers suggestions for drug education programs and a Rural Aging Network.

66. Liao, Winston, H. Hartoum, H. Rappaport, C. Harman, and

S. Abidi. "Drug Utilization Among the Rural Elderly." Triangle Park, North Carolina: International Fertility Research Program, 1979.

67. Lowe, George D. See entry number 759.

ECONOMICS, EMPLOYMENT AND WORK

68. Bauder, Ward W. See entry number 720.

69. Bradley, William. "Rural Poverty in an Urban State." In Paul K. H. Kim and C. P. Wilson (eds.), Toward Mental Health of the Rural Elderly. Washington, D. C.: University Press of America, 1981. Pp. 221-222.

Using New Jersey as an example, the author argues that even highly industrialized states have extensive rural poverty. Notes the need for more recognition of the problem and more effective programs to combat rural poverty.

70. Clemente, F., et. al. "The economic status of the aged." Madison, Wisconsin: University of Wisconsin, Center of Applied Sociology, 1973.

This longitudinal study of a rural Illinois community focuses on aged/non-aged differences in per capita income.

71. Coffin, Janet W., and Nelson L. LeRay. "Older Farm Operators and Their Farms." Economic Development Division; Economics, Statistics, and Cooperative Service; EDD Working Paper. Washington, D. C.: United States Department of Agriculture, November, 1979.

Reports on data from 1974 Census of Agriculture. Describes older farm operators and their farms, compares older and younger farmers, and discusses implications and research strategies.

72. Dudley, Phillip Lee Travers, Jr. "Grocery price differentials adverse to the elderly in rural communities." (Doctoral dissertation, University of Nebraska, Lincoln, Nebraska, 1981.) Dissertation Abstracts International, 42, 11, A, p.4893.

This study uses survey data collected randomly from 140 of 415 Nebraska grocery stores to determine if their pricing policies were adversely affecting their elderly customers. Four price indexes were used as dependent variables: dairy, meat, canned goods, and composite. No significant price differences were found between stores except for dairy products.

73. Dunsing, M. "Effect of Aging Upon the Income and Expenditures: A Longitudinal Study." Urbana, Illinois, University of Illinois, Department of Home Economics, 1972.

74. Gish, Pat B. "Unemployed Older Men, Dilapidated Rural Housing." Journal of Housing, 28:493-497 (1971).

   Describes Eastern Kentucky Home Repair, a federal-state-local project. Outlines successes, limitations of the program.

75. Goldstein, Sidney. See entry number 738.

76. Goudy, W. J., P. M. Keith, and E. A. Powers. "Older workers in small towns." Sociology Report #140. Ames, Iowa: Iowa State University, Occupational Involvement and Adaptation, 1977.

77. Heltsley, Mary E. "The Aged in Small Town, U.S.A." Journal of Home Economics, 68(4):47-50 (September, 1976).

   Presents data from extensive interviews with 20 persons over 75 years old living in small towns in southwest Iowa and having incomes of less than $1500. Examines respondents' difficulties in buying and preparing food and their reluctance to accept assistance from social agencies. Based on a larger study conducted in 1971.

78. Hirschl, Thomas A., and Gene F. Summer. "Cash transfers and the export base of small communities." Madison, Wisconsin: University of Wisconsin, Department of Rural Sociology, (May) 1981.

   Investigates the impact of social security benefits and elderly pension income on the economic structure of nonmetropolitan places. The authors find that social security payments are positively related to job creation and that retirees serve as an important industry.

79. Ilett, P. "Economic provisions for old age made by rural families." Knoxville, Tennessee: University of Tennessee, Department of Home Economics, 1971.

   An analysis of the economic plans made by rural families for old age.

80. Kim, Paul K. H. See entry number 151.

81. Kreps, Juanita M. See entry number 749.

82. Landis, Judson. "Factors Contributing to the Dependency of Rural Old People." Rural Sociology, 7:208-210 (June, 19-42).

   Examines difference between recipients and nonrecipients

of old age assistance in rural Iowa. Recepients were found to have the following characteristics: less education, more likely to live alone, and earlier retirement due to health reasons.

83. Larson, Donald K. See entry number 456.

84. Margolis, H. "Providing Part-time Jobs For Older Patients Hospitalized in Rural Areas." Hospital and Community Psychiatry, 31(9):634 (September, 1980).

A short description of an employment program for elderly patients of rural state hospitals. The therapeutic value of the work program is briefly discussed.

85. Martin, A. B. "Economic conditions of retired rural elderly in Tennessee." Washington, D. C.: United States Department of Agriculture, 1974.

86. Salamon, S., and V. Lockhart. "Land Ownership and the Position of Elderly in Farm Families." Human Organization, 39(4):324-331 (1980).

87. Salber, Eva J. "Three Interviews From Rural North Carolina." The Gerontologist, 20:421-426 (August, 1980).

An intimate description of the lives of three elderly North Carolina residents who live alone. Shows the elderly's ability to deal with difficult circumstances.

88. Saupe, W. E., et. al. "Wisconsin's older rural poor." Madison, Wisconsin: University of Wisconsin, College of Agricultural Life Sciences, December, 1975.

This report presents data on the economic and social status of low income rural Wisconsin households with heads aged 63 and older.

89. United States House, Select Committee on Aging, Subcommittee on Retirement Income and Employment. Employment needs of the rural and minority elderly. (94th Congress, 2nd Session, June 10th.) Washington, D. C.: United States Government Printing Office, 1976.

90. United States House, Select Committee on Aging. Avocational and employment needs of retired persons. (Hearing, February 11th.) Washington, D. C.: Untied States Government Printing Office, 1978.

91. United States House, Select Committee on Aging, Subcommittee on Retirement Income and Employment. Income status of the rural elderly. (Hearing, Swannanoa, North Carolina, 96th Congress, 2nd Session, Publication #96-253, August 29th.) Washington, D. C.: United States Government Printing Office, 1980.

92. United States Senate, Select Committee on Aging, Sub-committee on Retirement Income and Employment. Income status of the rural elderly. (Hearing, August 29th.) Washington, D. C.: United States Government Printing Offide, 1980.

93. Wickman, Peter M., and J. D. Yenerall. An Evaluation of Socio-Economic Problems Experienced by Senior Citizens in St. Lawrence County. Albany, New York: Office of Community Affairs, 1971.

94. Wilkinson, Carroll Wetzel. See entry number 178.

95. Wilkinson, Carroll Wetzel. See entry number 179.

96. Williams, William E. See entry number 672.

97. Wilson, Constance P. See entry number 674.

98. Youmans, E. Grant. "Socio-Economic Problems of Older Persons in Casey County, Kentucky." Bulletin #88. Lexington, Kentucky: Kentucky Agricultural Experiment Station, (March) 1960.

99. Youmans, E. Grant. "Economic Status and Attitudes of Older Men in Selected Rural and Urban Areas of Kentucky." Progress Report #105. Lexington, Kentucky: Agricultural Experiment Station, University of Kentucky, 1961.

EDUCATION AND TRAINING

100. Ansello, Edward F. "Antecedent Principles in Rural Gerontology Education." In Paul K. H. Kim and C. P. Wilson (eds.), Toward Mental Health of the Rural Elderly. Washington, D. C.: University Press of America, 1981. Pp. 1-14.

> Argues that if rural gerontological education is to better the lives of the rural elderly, it must be grounded in an understanding of the subculture of the rural elderly. It must begin with the acknowledgement that the needs of the rural elderly are different from those of urban elderly. Describes characteristics of the rural elderly as a subculture.

101. Ansello, Edward F., and Charles E. Cipolla (eds.). "Rural Aging and Education: Issues, Methods, and Models." Educational Gerontology, 5(4):343-447 (October-December, 19-80).

> Entire issue devoted to the rural elderly. Individual papers are annotated elsewhere in this bibliography.

102. Ater, E. Carolyn, and Carroll W. Baugh. "Consumer Education for the Rural Elderly." Educational Gerontology, 7:123-133 (September-October, 1981).

Discusses problems of the elderly consumer and describes a consumer education program in west Texas. Also reviews recent consumer education efforts as they relate to the elderly in general and the rural elderly in particular.

103. Bellism, James M., and Lawrence H. Poole. "Gerontology: The Center-based Approach." New Directions for Community Colleges, 7(3):15-22.

This article discusses the development of a community college based multidisciplinary gerontology center in a rural area. Describes the center's structure and functions and how it works to co-ordinate service provision to the rural elderly.

104. Clements, Claire. "The Rural Elderly and the Arts." In D. H. Hoffman, P. Greenberg and D. H. Fitzner (eds.), Lifelong Learning and the Visual Arts. Reston, Virginia: National Art Education Association, 1980. Pp. 62-66.

Describes Art for Older Americans, a program funded by the National Endowment for the Arts. The program taught crafts to 200 rural elderly residents of Gerogia. The program was conducted in county senior centers and met with enthusiasm from participants.

105. Ginsberg, Leon H. "Education for Social Work in Rural Settings." Social Work Education Reporter, 17:28-32, 60-61 (1969).

Reviews social problems of rural America, draws implications for social work practice, and outlines curriculum proposals for the education of rural practitioners.

106. Hoffman, Donald H. "Humanities and Arts Programs for Older Adults in Rural Settings." In Paul K. H. Kim and C. P. Wilson (eds.), Toward Mental Health of the Rural Elderly. Washington, D. C.: University Press of America, 1981. Pp. 379-388.

Argues that the arts and humanities offer many benefits to the elderly and need to be more heavily utilized to help the rural elderly by lessening the negative effects of retirement and aging. Outlines the development and implimentation of an arts program in a rural area.

107. Kim, Paul K. H. See entry number 151.

108. Kim, Paul K. H. See entry number 65.

109. Kim, Paul K. H. "Toward Rural Gerontological Education: Rationale and Model." Educational Gerontology, 5(4):387-397 (1980).

The author argues that the rural elderly are a "minority group" and have been largely ignored in areas of
gerontological training and research and public policy
and planning. Reviews unresolved issues of the 1970's
in the field of aging and proposes an educational model
for the 1980's that would attend to the problems facing the rural elderly.

110. Liley, Floyd Wilbur. See entry number 27.

111. Lowe, Laura Gertrude. "The research and development
of multimedia leisure-learning packages for the rural elderly." (Doctoral dissertation, University of Oregon, Eugene,
Oregon, November, 1980.) Dissertation Abstracts International, 41, 5, A, p.2288.

This dissertation reports on the development and field
testing of two leisure-learning packages designed to
provide education/recreation activities for the elderly. These packages incorporated the multi-media
delivery system approach. The researcher reports
the packages were successful.

112. Mickey, Callie Parker. See entry number 605.

113. Monk, Abraham. "Education and the Rural Aged." Educational Gerontology, 2:147-156 (April, 1977).

Proposes an ecological-consultative continuum of education as an outreach program which would first re-
solve essential functioning matters for rural elderly
and then move on to resocialization and social com-
petence.

114. Murray, Martha Sadowski. "Variables affecting the
reading preferences of institutionalized versus noninstitutionalized rural older adults." (Doctoral dissertation,
Adult Education, North Carolina State University, Raleigh,
North Carolina, 1979.) Dissertation Abstracts International, 40, 2, A, p.1815.

Compares reading preferences of institutionalized versus noninstitutionalized rural older adults. A sample
of 16 institutionalized and 13 noninstitutionalized
elderly was studied. Institutionalized elderly read
mainly to pass the time while the noninstitutionalized
aged read to learn.

115. Overland, Shirley. See entry number 624.

116. Price, William F. "Developing the Resources of the
Rural Elderly Through Education." Educational Gerontology,
5:423-427 (October, 1980).

Discusses the inclusion of a serious, academic component as well as a recreational one in education programs for the rural elderly. Gives as an example a program by North County Community College of Saranac Lake, New York.

117. Wilkinson, Carroll Wetzel. See entry number 178.

118. Wilkinson, Carroll Wetzel. See entry number 179.

119. Wilson, Constance P. See entry number 674.

FAMILY

120. Britton, Joseph H., and Jean O. Britton. "The Middle-Aged and Older Rural Person and His Family." In E. Grant Youmans (ed.), Older Rural Americans. Lexington, Kentucky: University of Kentucky Press, 1967. Pp. 44-74.

A general discussion of the rural older person's role and integration in the family. Takes a developmental approach to the family focusing on changes in the interaction between rural adults and their families throughout the middle and older years.

121. Britton, Joseph H. "Reaction to Family Environments and Friendships." In R. C. Atchley with Thomas O. Byerts (eds.), Rural Environments and Aging. Washington, D. C.: Gerontological Society, 1975. Pp. 91-94.

Notes both strengths and weaknesses of the paper, "Family Relationships and Friendships", by Powers, Keith, and Goudy.

122. Bultena, Gordon L. See entry number 145.

123. Bultena, Gordon L. See entry number 725.

124. Coward, Raymond T. (ed.) Rural Families Across the Life Span: Implications for Community Programming. West Lafayette, Indiana: Indiana Cooperative Extension Service, 1977.

A collection of papers dealing with families in rural communities. While many of the papers do not deal specifically with the elderly, they have implications for rural aging and the aged. Topics covered include: service delivery, demographic structure of the family, family programs, middle-aged and older families and social policy.

125. Decker, James T. See entry number 412.

126. Deimling, Gary T. See entry number 339.

127. Ilett, P. See entry number 79.

128. Key, William H. See entry number 745.

129. Kim, Paul K. H. See entry number 151.

130. Kivett, Vira R. See entry number 41.

131. Learner, R. Max, and Vira R. Kivett. "Adults and Their In-Laws: An Assessment of Attitudes and the Quality of Relationships." Paper presented at the Annual Meeting of the Gerontological Society of America (San Deigo, California; November, 1980).

>A study of the characteristics of in-law relationships and comparison between in-laws and blood kin for a sample of aged 65 and over nonmetropolitan area residents.

132. Mahoney, Kevin J. See entry number 762.

133. Powers, Edward A., Patricia M. Keith, and Willis J. Goudy. "Family Relationships and Friendships." In R. C. Atchley with Thomas O. Byerts (eds.), Rural Environments and Aging. Washington, D. C.: The Gerontological Society, 1975. p. 67.

>An extensive review of the literature on the family relationships and friendships of the rural elderly. Covers work on family patterns (residence, proximity and contact with siblings, assistance and helping patterns, attitudes of filial responsibility) friendship patterns (contact with friends and neighbors, confidants, assistance) and the policy implications and research needs of this area.

134. Powers, Edward A., Patricia M. Keith, and Willis J. Goudy. "Family Networks of the Rural Aged." In Raymond T. Coward and W. M. Smith, Jr. (eds.), The Family in Rural Society. Boulder, Colorado: Westview Press, 1981. Pp. 199-217.

>A review of the literature on the family patterns of older rural adults. Examines rural-urban differences in areas such as residence, proximity and contact with children, siblings and family, assistance, and helping patterns. Also, data from a 1960's study of age 50 and over males living in small Iowa towns are analyzed.

135. Sauer, William J. See entry number 775.

136. Scott, Jean Pearson. See entry number 401.

137. Taylor, Charles. "The Open Hearth or the Open Road: The Dilemma of the Older Family." Paper presented at the

Symposium on Rural Families Across the Life Span and the Implications for Community Programming at the Indiana Cooperative Extension Service (West Lafayette, Indiana; May, 1977). Pp. 107-117.

> Addresses the question of the desirability of the elderly remaining in rural areas versus moving to other places.

138. Wilkinson, Carroll Wetzel. See entry number 179.

139. Youmans, E. Grant. See entry number 798.

GENERAL

140. Adams, David L. "Who Are The Rural Aged." In Robert C. Atchley with Thomas O. Byerts (eds.), Rural Environments and Aging. Washington, D. C.: Gerontological Society, 1975. Pp. 11-21.

> Discusses the problems attendant to classifying individuals as rural or elderly. Stresses the need to examine variables from past, present, and future environments of the rural aged.

141. Atchley, Robert C. "Introduction." In Robert C. Atchley with Thomas O. Byerts (eds.), Rural Environments and Aging. Washington, D. C.: Gerontological Society, 1975. Pp. 1-9.

> Discusses some definitions of rural and presents a brief summary of each of the chapters in this book.

142. Atchley, Robert C. with Thomas O. Byerts (eds.), Rural Environments and Aging. Washington, D. C.: Gerontological Society, 1975.

> Proceedings of a conference sponsored by the Gerontological Society and held in Lexington, Kentucky. Basic information on the rural elderly. Includes chapters on the following: culture, life style, and social environments, family relationships and friendships, housing, community facilities and social services, nutrition, health care, and transportation.

143. Barron, Milton L. "Survey of the Rural Aged." In Milton L Barron (ed.), The Aging American: An Introduction to Social Gerontology and Geriatics. New York, New York: Thomas Y. Crowell Co., 1961.

144. Britton, Jean O., et. al. Personality Changes in Aging: A Longitudinal Study of Community Residents. New York, New York: Springer Publishing Co., 1972.

> A nine year longitudinal study of some 500 aged resi-

dents of a small rural Pennsylvania community. Focuses on personal and social norms and expectations for behavior.

145. Bultena, G. L. "Adaptations to aging in small towns." Ames, Iowa: Iowa State University, Department of Sociology and Anthropology, 1974.

A longitudinal study of the family and community integration of older people living in a small Iowa town. The authors note a significant decline in the elderly's health, income, mobility, and social contacts although morale levels remained high.

146. Copp, James H. "The rural aged: what we need to know." College Station, Texas: A. & M. University, 1980.

147. Coward, R. T., and G. R. Lee (eds.), Every Third Elder: Aging in Rural Environments. New York, New York: Springer Publishing Co. (in press), 1983.

148. Fleming, Arthur S. "Reports of the special concerns session", for the White House Conference on Aging, 1971. The Rural and The Poor Elderly. Washington, D. C.: United States Government Printing Office, 1972.

149. Harootyan, Robert A. "Growing older in rural America: demographic trends and social policy issues", Prepared for the United States Senate, Special Committee on Aging. The Nation's Rural Elderly, Part 7, Denver, Colorado. (94th Congress, 2nd Session, March 23rd.) Washington, D. C.: United States Government Printing Office, 1977.

A series of hearings held in Iowa, South Dakota, and Nebraska on the rural elderly. Part 7 is especially noteworthy and includes a number of papers on the rural elderly.

150. Hoffman, Donald H., and Headlee Lamprey. Rural Aging. Lexington, Kentucky: Council on Aging - University Extension, University of Kentucky, (November) 1979.

A collection of papers presented at a seminar on Rural Aging held at the University of Kentucky.

151. Kim, Paul K. H., and H. Lamprey. A Bibliography on Aspects of Mental Health in Rural Aging. Lexington, Kentucky: Mental Health and Rural Gerontology Project, University of Kentucky, Gerontology Publication Series, 1979-1, 1979.

Contains 553 citations to materials concerning the rural elderly. The title is misleading in that the bibliography covers nine broad subject areas besides mental health including: demographics, economics, housing, physical health, human services, social ac-

tivities, transportation, general, and foreign. The
organization of this bibliography makes it a bit awk-
ward to use and not all the citations refer specifically to the rural elderly.

152. Kim, Paul K. H., and Constance P. Wilson (eds.), Toward Mental Health of the Rural Elderly. Washington, D. C.:
University Press of America, 1981.

Chapters are by professionals in the field and focus
on the problems and treatment of the rural elderly.
Problems are presented in three parts: basic philoso-
phy, problems and their causes, and problems in service delivery. Individual articles are annotated in
appropriate subject headings in this bibliography.

153. Kohls, J. M., and G. T. Hudson. "The Older Citizens
In Three Arkansas Communities." The Station Bulletin. Fay-
etteville, Arkansas: The Agricultural Experiment Station,
(May) 1979.

An examination of the self-perceived needs of the elderly.

154. Kutner, B., D. Fanshel, A. M. Togo, and T. S. Langner.
Five Hundred Over Sixty: A Community Study of Aging. New
York, New York: Russell Sage, 1956.

A detailded study of five hundred aged sixty and over
residents of a rural central Pennsylvania community.

155. Lassey, William R., Marie L. Lassey, Gary R. Lee, Naomi
Lee, Edward O. Moe, Raymond T. Coward, John E. Kushman, James
Fujii, and Victor A. Christopherson. "Research and Public
Service With the Rural Elderly." Proceedings of a Conference
at the Western Rural Development Center, Oregon State Univer-
sity (Corvallis, Oregon; October, 1980).

A collection of papers on the rural elderly dealing
with a number of topics. Individual papers are annotated elsewhere in this bibliography and cover topics
such as: needs assessment, alcohol use, research
priorities, rural-urban residence, and research-based
programming.

156. Lozier, John, and Ronald Althouse. "Social Enforcement
of Behavior Toward Elders in an Appalachian Mountain Settle-
ment." The Gerontologist, 14:69-80 (February, 1974).

A study of several case histories of aging individuals
from West Virginia investigating societal expectations
regarding treatment of elderly persons.

157. McKain, W. C. Aging in Rural Connecticut. Springfield,
Virginia: National Technical Information Service, United

States Department of Commerce, 1973.

An overview of the number and characteristics of elderly persons living in rural Connecticut.

158. Marshall, Douglas G. "Older People in Rural Development Areas in Wisconsin." In Ruth E. Albrecht (ed.), Aging
in a Changing Society. Gainesville, Florida: University
of Florida Press, Institute of Gerontological Series Vol. 11,
1962. Pp. 47-66.

159. Morrison, D. E., et. al. "Personal Adjustment Among
Older Persons." Bulletin #21. South Dakota: South Dakota
Agricultural Experiment Station, 1958.

This report examines the relationship between personal
adjustment among the elderly living in a rural South
Dakota community and their contact with family and
friends.

160. National Council on the Aging. Triple Jeopardy-Myth
or Reality. Washington, D. C.: National Council on Aging,
(April) 1972.

A selection of papers delivered at National Council on
Aging regional meetings. One of these papers deals
with the rural elderly.

161. National Council on the Aging, Inc. "A Look at Rural
Realities." Perspective on Aging, 7(1):(February, 1978).

162. Newhart, Robert L. "Growing Older in Rural America."
Proceedings from a symposium of the 23rd Annual Meeting of
the Western Gerontological Society, 1977. Pp. 23-24.

163. Northeast Regional Center for Rural Development. "The
Proceedings of the Workshop on Rural Gerontology Research in
the Northeast." Publication #14. Ithaca, New York: Northeast Regional Center for Rural Research in the Northeast,
Cornell University, May, 1977.

A collection of papers on the rural elderly dealing
with a number of topics. Individual papers are annotated elsewhere in this bibliography.

164. Pihlblad, C. T. See entry number 9.

165. Redding, Leonard F. "Rural Elderly: The Ignored American." Paper presented to the Regional Conference of the
National Council on Aging (Charleston, South Carolina; April
25, 1975).

166. Rose, Arnold M. "Perspectives on the Rural Aged." In
E. Grant Youmans (ed.), Older Rural Americans. Lexington,
Kentucky: University of Kentucky Press, 1967. Pp. 6-21.

Analyzes the rural elderly using three sets of factors: aging in American society, characteristics of rural life, and characteristics of rural life 60 years ago when today's elderly were in their formative years.

167. Rural America Staff. "Rural America Factsheet: The Elderly." Rural America Factsheet #5. Washington, D. C.: Rural America Factsheet, 1345 Connecticut Avenue, Northwest, 1978.

168. Schooler, Kermit K. See entry number 776.

169. Sotomayor, Martha. The Rural Elderly. Washington, D. C.: Rural Development Service, United States Department of Agriculture, 1977.

170. Sotomayor, Martha. See entry number 473.

171. Stafford, P. B. Old Age in a Small Town: Semantics and Pragmatics. Bloomington, Indiana: South Central Community Mental Health Center, 1978.

172. United States Department of Housing and Urban Development, Division on Aging. A Re-Study of 1,700 Older Persons After 5 Years. Columbia, Missouri: University of Missouri, 1973.

173. United States House, Committee on Government Operations. "The People Left Behind - The Rural Elderly." Geriatrics, June 22, 1974.

174. United States Senate, Special Committee on Aging. Senate Hearings on Older Americans in Rural Areas, I-XII, Special Committee on Aging. (91st Congress, 1st Session.) Washington, D. C.: United States Government Printing Office, 1969.

175. United States Senate, Special Committee on Aging. Development in Aging. (95th Congress, 1st Session.) Washington, D. C.: United States Government Printing Office, 1976.

176. Watkins, Dennis A., and Charles O. Crawford (eds.). "Rural Gerontology Research in the Northeast." Proceeding from a workshop at Pennsylvania State University, State Colege, Pennsylvania, (July, 1978).

177. 1971 White House Conference on Aging. "Older Americans in Rural and Small Towns." In L. H. Ginsberg (ed.), Social Work in Rural Communities. New York, New York: Council on Social Work Education, 1976. Pp. 95-98.

Reports on a conference session on the special needs of rural and small town aged. Presents data and recommendations for action.

An Annotated Bibliography

178. Wilkinson, Carroll Wetzel. Comprehensive Annotated
Bibliography on the Rural Aged, 1975 - 1978. Morgantown,
West Virginia: Gerontology Center, West Virginia University,
1978.

     An annotated bibliography of some 145 publications
     dealing with the rural elderly. The coverage is some-
     what limited by the fact that most of the articles
     were published in a three year period. While many of
     the citations are not actually annotated, this work
     is well organized. Citations are annotated alphabetic-
     ally in a 31 page author index and listed again in a
     21 page subject index.

179. Wilkinson, Carroll Wetzel. Aging in Rural America: A
Comprehensive Annotated Bibliography 1975 - 1981. Morgantown, West Virginia: Gerontology Center, West Virginia University, 1982.

     An updated and expanded version of Wilkinson's earlier
     bibliography. This work follows the format she esta-
     blished earlier listing annotations alphabetically in
     a 71 page author index and listing them again in a 45
     page subject index. The subject index has 24 sections.
     Many of the annotations are rather more like abstracts
     giving abundant information on the scope and findings
     of the particular publication. This work is somewhat
     limited by its time coverage but otherwise in an ex-
     cellent bibliography.

180. Windley, Paul G. "Reaction to Who Are the Rural Aged?"
In Robert C. Atchley with Thomas O. Byerts (eds.), Rural En-
vironments and Aging. Washington, D. C.: Gerontological
Society, 1975. Pp. 23-26.

     Urges caution regarding two positions taken by David
     Adams in his paper, "Who Are the Rural Aged?" Notes
     Adams' lack of specificity.

181. Yenerall, Joseph D., and Sondra F. Haynes. The Rural
Aged in America: An Annotated Bibliography. Albany,
New York: Institute for Public Policy Alternatives, State
University of New York, 1975.

     A somewhat dated annotated bibliography of publications
     on the elderly. Many of the citations refer to works
     that do not specifically focus on the rural aged. In-
     cludes eight chapters with works listed alphabetically
     in each chapter. Topics covered include: perspectives
     on the rural elderly, work, leisure and retirement,
     family and kinship, housing, transportation, health
     status, health care, and programs and services. There
     is no general author index.

182. Youmans, E. Grant (ed.). Older Rural Americans. Lexington, Kentucky: University of Kentucky Press, 1967.

25

Presents a sociological perspective on older persons living in rural America. Chapters on social roles, health, social and economic conditions, subcultures, and programs for the rural elderly. Individual articles are annotated under the appropriate headings in this bibliography.

183. Youmans, E. Grant. "The Rural Aged." Annals of the American Academy of Political and Social Science, 429:81-90 (January, 1977).

Objective and subjective conditions of life of the rural elderly are described. Rural-urban comparisons are made. Stresses the need for research and suggests solutions.

HEALTH, MENTAL

184. Ballantine, John R. "Rural Community Mental Health Centers: Today and Tomorrow." In Paul K. H. Kim and C. P. Wilson (eds.), Toward Mental Health of the Rural Elderly. Washington, D. C.: University Press of America, 1981. Pp. 389-393.

Outlines the development of rural mental health services in Kentucky from 1963 until the present. Discusses types of services, percentage of elderly being served, and problems the elderly have in accessing available services. Offers suggestions for solving these problems.

185. Berry, J. In Paul K. H. Kim and C. P. Wilson (eds.), Toward Mental Health and Rural Gerontology. Lexington, Kentucky: University of Kentucky, College of Social Work (in press) 1983.

186. Bognar, Bela J. "Predicted Mental Health Vulnerability Among Aged Who Live in Semi-Rural Communities." Paper presented at the Annual Meeting of the Gerontological Society of America (Washington, D. C.; November, 1979).

187. Britton, Joseph H. "Assessment of Services for the Aged in Rural Communities." Journal of Gerontology, 13:67-69 (1958).

This article focuses on the mental health and use of mental health services of older adults from almost 500 households located in a rural Pennsylvania community. Data was collected from the elderly and agency professionals serving them. The findings are largely descriptive.

188. Casper, Max, and Dan Rubenstein. "Rural Elderly and Mental Health: Educating the Rural Mental Health Social

Worker." Paper presented at the Annual Program Meeting of the Council on Social Work Education (Boston, Massachusetts; March, 1979).

189. Casper, Max, and Dan Rubenstein. "Mental health of the rural elderly: social problem or untapped resource?" Syracuse, New York: School of Social Work, Syracuse University, 1979.

190. Flax, James W., Morton O. Wagenfeld, Ruby E. Ivens, and Robert J. Weiss. Mental Health and Rural America: An Overview and Annotated Bibliography. Rockville, Maryland: National Institute on Mental Health, 1979.

 An annotated bibliography of some 393 materials on mental health and rural America. Only a few of these deal directly with the elderly. However, the annotations are quite extensive and would be useful to student's of rural environments.

191. Harel, Zev, Robert N. Sollod, and Bela J. Bognar. "Predictors of Mental Health Among Semi-Rural Aged." The Gerontologist, 22(6):499-504 (December, 1982).

 This study examines correlates of mental health and levels of mental health vulnerability for a sample of 1,008 elderly individuals living in a "semi-rural" Ohio county. Independent variables used in this research were demographic characteristics, social integration, health and functional status, and socioeconomic status. Many of these measures were found to be associated with mental health.

192. Kim, Paul K. H. See entry number 151.

193. Kim, Paul K. H. See entry number 152.

194. Mesmer, Roger E. G. "A Community Psychiatry Program in a Rural State Hospital." Hospital and Community Psychiatry, 22:248-251 (August, 1971).

 A history and description of a community psychiatry program which helped start the Warren, Pennsylvania Senior Center.

195. Rathbone-McCuan, E. See entry number 630.

196. Rosen, Catherine E. See entry number 272.

197. Rosen, S. See entry number 273.

198. Saltzman, Ben N. "Mental Health and the Rural Aging." The Journal of the Arkansas Medical Society, 68:131-133 (September, 1971).

A physician contemplates the many problems of mental
and emotional health of the elderly. The problems are
often exacerbated by a rural environment because of
isolation, lack of productive activities, and a short-
age of professional help.

199. Scheidt, Rick J. "Psychosocial Environmental Predic-
tors of the Mental Health of the Small-town Rural Elderly."
In Paul K. H. Kim and C. P. Wilson (eds.), Toward Mental
Health of the Rural Elderly. Washington, D. C.: University
Press of America, 1981. Pp. 5-80.

Reports on a 1978 study of 1,000 elderly residents of
18 small Kansas towns. Assesses the impact of demographic, psychosocial, and ecological/architectural
variables on 17 dimensions of well-being. Also examines a number of other aspects of respondent behavior and attitudes.

200. Scheidt, Rick J., and R. J. Windley. "Differentiating
Rural Contexts: Impact Upon the Mental Health of Small-town
Elderly." Paper presented at the Annual Meeting of the Gerontological Society of America (San Diego, California; November, 1980).

One of the few studies to examine the elderly living
in a range of small town/rural environments. Focuses
on a number of indicators of mental health.

201. Task Panel Report on Mental Health of the Elderly and
Task Panel Report on Rural Mental Health. Prepared for the
President's Commission on Mental Health. Washington, D. C.:
United States Government Printing Office, 1972.

202. Windley, Paul G., and Rick J. Scheidt. "An Ecological
Model of Mental Health Among Small-town Rural Elderly."
Journal of Gerontology, 37(2):235-242 (March, 1982).

This article presents data on the relationship between
three sets of environmental variables (ecological/
architectural, psychosocial, and personal) on the
mental health of almost 1,000 non-institutionalized
elderly living in rural Kansas towns. Psychosocial
variables were found to partially mediate the relationship between the ecological/architectural and
personal variables and mental health.

HEALTH, PHYSICAL

203. Brown, Martha Susan. See entry number 493.

204. Crase, Darrell. See entry number 2.

205. D'Elia, Gabrielle, and Roland Folse. "Medical Problems
of the Elderly in Nonmetropolitan Illinois." Journal of

Gerontology, 33:681-687 (1978).

This study utilizes data from the patient records of
965 elderly living in a nonmetropolitan area. Data
on patient status, presenting problems, principal
diagnoses, reasons for visit, and disposition are examined. The authors argue that although variations
exist, the medical problems observed in the rural
elderly are similar to those found among the elderly
in general.

206. Dahlsten, J., and J. C. Shank. "Chronic and Acute Dis-
ease Problems in Rural Nursing Home Patients." Journal of
the American Geriatric Society, 27:112-116 (March, 1979).

A study of 66 rural Iowa nursing home patients, three-
quarters of whom were over age 75. Identified relative frequency of chronic and acute health conditions
of these patients. The most frequent chronic conditions were senility and circulatory disorders while
genito-urinary problems topped the acute condition
list.

207. Edwards, J. N. See entry number 443.

208. Ehrlich, Phyllis Diane. See entry number 341.

209. Ellenbogen, Bert L. See entry number 736.

210. Escher, M. C. See entry number 64.

211. Franck, Phyllis. "A Survey of Health of Older Adults
in Northwest Johnson County, Iowa." Nursing Research, 28(6):
360-264.

Reports findings from a survey of elderly Iowa residents' health perceptions and needs.

212. Kim, Paul K. H. See entry number 151.

213. McCoy, John L. See entry number 760.

214. McMillen, Marilyn. "Community health profile of West
Liberty, West Virginia." Kent, Ohio: Department of Sociology, Kent State University, 1972.

The "Portage Health Survey" is used to examine the
health status of residents of a rural community. Explores use of medical facilities and attitudes toward
health services.

215. Paringer, Lynn, et. al. Health Status and Use of Medical Services: Evidence on the Poor, Black and the Rural
Elderly. Washington, D. C.: Urban Institute, 1979.

This monograph examines the health status and medical service utilization among the poor, black, and rural elderly. Considerable differences are found between these three categories of the aged. Income and race but not place of residence were found to be significantly associated with health status. Black, low income, and rural elderly underutilized medical care services given their level of need.

216. Pomerville, Julie. "The Health Status of the Rural Elderly: Evidence From 2 Rural Villages." Paper presented at the 21st Annual Meeting of the New York State Sociological Association at Eisenhower College (Seneca Falls, New York; October, 1973).

217. Richard, Jane Ann. "Social class correlates of the perceived health status of the rural elderly." (Doctoral dissertation, Ohio State University, Columbus, Ohio, 1981.) Dissertation Abstracts International, 42, 1-2, A, p.874.

This study reports findings on the effect of socioeconomic factors on the perception of health status for a sample of 246 elderly Californians living in four rural counties. While income and retirement were found to be significantly related to health status perception, these variables explained a very small amount of the variance in the dependent variable.

218. Schooler, Kermit K. "Residential physical environment and health of the aged." Final report, U.S.P.H.S. Grant EC 00191. Waltham, Maine: Brandeis University, Florence Heller School for Advanced Studies in Social Welfare, 1970.

219. Wilkinson, Carroll Wetzel. See entry number 178.

220. Wilkinson, Carroll Wetzel. See entry number 179.

221. Youmans, E. Grant. See entry number 793.

222. Youmans, E. Grant. See entry number 799.

223. Youmans, E. Grant. See entry number 803.

224. Youmans, E. Grant, and Donald K. Larson. "Health status and needs: a study of older people in Powell County, Kentucky." RS - 52. Lexington, Kentucky: Department of Sociology, University of Kentucky, Agricultural Experiment Station, April, 1977.

Assesses the health status and needs of 399 older residents of Powell County, Kentucky. Data are presented on self perceptions of physical, mental, and social well-being.

HEALTH CARE

225. Ahearn, Mary C. See entry number 714.

226. Baines, Elizabeth Murrow. See entry number 373.

227. Ballanger, Judith. "Lend-A-Hand Lives Up to Its Name."
Appalachia, 4(9):15-19 (1971).

    Describes a home health care service to primarily eld-
    erly patients in Knox County, Kentucky.

228. Ballantine, John R. See entry number 184.

229. Balswick, Jack O., Harold Bronfin, Ira E. Robinson,
and Carol A. Gersnehl. "Medical Services for the Aged in
Rural Areas." Nursing Homes, 15-17 (December, 1970).

    A study in Georgia assessing the impact of three feder-
    al acts on nursing homes and on rural health care ser-
    vices. Questionnaires were mailed to 210 licenced
    nursing homes.

230. Bell, Bill D. "Mobile Medical Care to the Elderly:
An Evaluation." The Gerontologist, 15:100-103 (1975).

    Describes and evaluates a statewide mobile program of
    health care delivery to the rural elderly of Arkansas.

231. Bible, Bond L. "Health Care in Rural Areas." Paper
presented at the Annual Meeting of the Association of Southern Agricultural Workers (Atlanta, Georgia; February, 1973).

    Outlines special problems of providing rural health
    care. Makes recommendations to help alleviate those
    problems.

232. Brandt, Edna J., Helena M. Haley, Lenora B. Mahoney,
and Carmel A. McKay. "A Home Nursing Service in a Rural
County." American Journal of Public Health, 51:1294-1304
(September, 1961).

    Describes a home nursing service in a rural county in
    California, how it began and grew, problems it en-
    countered, and possibilities for the future.

233. Brown, David L. See entry number 724.

234. Brown, T. E., and R. M. Learner. "Community-Based Long
Term Care For Low Income Rural Elderly." Paper presented at
the Annual Meeting of the Gerontological Society of America
(Toronto, Canada; November, 1981).

    Describes a community long term care project establish-
    ed to determine the feasibility of case management and

31

expanded community services for long term health care at home. Particular attention is paid to the process of setting up such a system and identifying the effects of project services on client outcomes, service utilization, and costs. Also discusses problems in implementing services in a rural area and outlines implications for policy planners and practitioners.

235. Britton, Joseph H. See entry number 187.

236. Casper, Max. See entry number 188.

237. Clements, G. "A Geriatric Day Hospital Serving a Rural Community." Nursing Times (London), 64(27):908-909 (1968).

Describes the development, staffing, daily routine, and patient profile of a geriatric day hospital located in a rural area. The author argues problems in areas such as transportation have been overcome and that the hospital has been a success.

238. Coogan, Mercy Hardie. "Yes, You Can Go Home Again: South Carolina's Community Long Term Care Project." Appalachia, 14:28-38 (July-August, 1981).

This article describes a community long term care project for the elderly operating in three rural South Carolina counties. The program, first funded in 1978 by the Appalachian Regional Commission, offers a wide array of services to 335 clients including: medical day care, respite care, home-delivered meals, transportation, medical social services, mental health, and physical therapy.

239. Costello, T. Patrick. See entry number 731.

240. Cozart, E. S. See entry number 358.

241. Crase, Darrell. See entry number 2.

242. Davenport, Joseph, III, and Judith A. Davenport. "Health-Related Social Services for the Rural Elderly: Problems and Opportunities." Social Perspectives, 5:36-41 (December, 1977).

Shows how a state university established an agency providing health related services to rural elderly while also training social work students. Found rural health problems of elderly exacerbated by problems specific to rural areas such as lack of public transportation. Many of rural elderly were suspicious of outsiders and found it difficult to accept help.

243. Deimling, Gary T. See entry number 339.

244. Doeksen, Gerold A., and Shevu-Eng Webb. "Applied Rural Transportation Research for Rural Decisionmakers." Paper presented at the Annual Meeting of the Rural Sociological Society (Burlington, Vermont; August, 1979).

> Illustrates the use of research findings by decision-makers. Describes an application of an emergency medical service study and a program which will allow cost estimates of transportation systems.

245. Dunkley, Russell A., Candida J. Lutes, Judith N. Wooten, and Robert A. Kooken. "Therapy Approaches With Rural Elders." In S. S. Sargent (ed.), Nontraditional Therapy and Counseling With the Aging. New York, New York: Springer Publishing Co., 1980. Pp. 74-99.

> Presents an analysis of alternative strategies for providing psychological services to the rural elderly. Approaches considered include: community education, working with other service providers, workshops, and community based meetings.

246. Egli, Daniel. "The Role of the Clinical Psychologist in the Rural Nursing Home Setting." In Paul K. H. Kim and C. P. Wilson (eds.), Toward Mental Health of the Rural Elderly. Washington, D. C.: University Press of America, 1981. Pp. 369-378.

> Presents statistics on nursing homes and a literature review of issues in rural mental health service delivery. Discusses the role of the clinical psychologist in rural nursing homes.

247. Ehrlich, Phyllis Diane. See entry number 341.

248. Fitzwilliams, Jeanette. "Unmasking problems in rural health planning. Rural Development Research Report No. 11. Washington, D. C.: United States Department of Agriculture, Economics, Statistics, and Cooperatives Service, 1979.

> Argues that needs of the rural elderly would be better served if health statistics were separated into smaller geographic segments and there was more flexibility in regulations and funding formulas.

249. Friedman, Emily. "Little Hospital Has Big Ideas." Hospitals, 54(22):89-94 (1980).

> Describes a small northern Wisconsin Hospital's expansion into health care provision for the elderly.

250. Gibbs, Tyson. "Rural Elderly Health Care Seeking Behavior." NCBA Quarterly Contact, 5(1):4(Spring, 1982).

251. Gombeski, William Robert, Jr., and Michael H. Smolensky.

"Non-Emergency Health Transportation Needs of the Rural Elderly." The Gerontologist, 20(4):452-456 (1980).

> A description and analysis of health related transportation needs. Data collected via an open-ended interview questionnaire administered to 99 elderly residents of Houston County, Texas showed the following variables to be related to type of transportation used: age, race, marital status, and owning a telephone or automobile.

252. House, Gail. "Delivery of In-Home Care to the Rural Elderly: A Viable Alternative?" Generations (Western Gerontological Society), Fall:16-17 (1977).

> A brief description of an AoA funded program to bring in-home care to the rural aged in West Texas.

253. Johnson, David Pittman, and Stephanie Waller. "Cognitive Treatment for the Elderly With Social Status Problems." In Paul K. H. Kim and C. P. Wilson (eds.), Toward Mental Health of the Rural Elderly. Washington, D. C.: University Press of America, 1981. Pp. 351-367.

> Identifies major social status problems of the elderly. Presents cognitive theory as a means of combating the undesirable social status assigned to the elderly. Final section is devoted to delivery of services to the rural aged.

254. Jones, Ann A., Peter W. Shaughnessy, and James D. Lubitz. "Experimental Programs Provide Long Term Care in Rural Hospitals." Generations (Western Gerontological Society), Fall:14-15 (1977).

> A brief discussion of experimental programs designed to better utilize rural hospitals by involving them in the provision of institutional and non-institutional long-term care and as focal points for outreach programs.

255. Kretz, S. E. "Health Care for the Rural Elderly: Implications of Trends in the Distribution of Rural Physicians." Paper presented at the Annaul Meeting of the Gerontological Society of America (San Diego, California; November, 1980).

> Explores the barriers and problems associated with developing rural primary care physician practices. Argues that specific policy interventions are needed to prevent a greater shortage of doctors in rural areas and suggests specific policy actions.

256. Lane, N. M. "Rural Clinics and 'Swing Beds' May Solve Health Care Dilemma." Perspective on Aging, 7(1):14-15 (1978).

Discusses the use of local health clinics as a strategy to meet basic health care needs of the rural elderly.

257. Learner, R. Max, T. E. Brown, and D. K. Pierce. "Disabled Rural Elderly: Characteristics and Long Term Care Service Needs." Paper presented at the Annual Meeting of the
Gerontological Society of America, (Toronto, Canada; November,
1981).

This paper presents initial findings from a longitudinal study of community-based alternatives to nursing
home care for a sample of disabled elderly living in
South Carolina. The sample was found to have considerable functional impairment and to rely largely on family not community services for support. Long term care
service operation in rural areas is discussed.

258. Linstrom, R. C. See entry number 589.

259. McMillen, Marilyn. See entry number 214.

260. Maki, W. R. "Service Delivery Alternatives in Rural
Development." Research Work Unit/Project Description Pro-
Press Report MIN-14-082. St. Paul, Minnesota: Department
of Agriculture and Applied Economics and Agriculture, Experiment Station, University of Minnesota, 1975.

Reviews alternative health care services in Minnesota.
Notes the need for improvement in traditional health
care systems.

261. Margolis, H. See entry number 84.

262. Mesmer, Roger E. G. See entry number 194.

263. Mountain States Health Corporation. Patient Activated
Care for the Rural Elderly. Boise, Idaho: Mountain States
Health Corporation, 1981.

A manual for planners and others interested in initiat-
ing self-care programs for older adults living in rural
communities. The book has three sections: program
development guide, session guidelines, and an evaluation guide. Also includes sample forms, questionnaires,
charts, etc.

264. Myllymaki, Judy. "Montana Rural Social Service Deli-
very System." Evaluation Report, Project Share, SHR000021.
Rockville, Maryland: Project Share, P.O. Box 309, SHR000021,
Rockville, Maryland, 20852, 1972.

Describes and evaluates a health system providing services to a sparsely populated area of Montana. Data
from interviews with agency personnel and 693 elderly
residents.

265. Oliver, David B. See entry number 502.

266. Oyler, R. L. "Utilization of Physicians Service By Rural Aged Populations." Paper presented at the Annual Meeting of the Gerontological Society of America (November, 1967).

267. Paringer, Lynn. See entry number 215.

268. Parkinson, Larry. See entry number 627.

269. Pickard, Larry. "Long Term Care and the Rural Aged." In Paul K. H. Kim and P. C. Wilson (eds.), <u>Toward Mental Health of the Rural Elderly</u>. Washington, D. C.: University Press of America, 1981. Pp. 275-281.

> Emphasizes the advantages of rural areas for establish-ing long term care programs. Financial resources may be more limited than in urban areas but the author suggests that this may be offset by the strength of other resources including; family, friends, local organizations, the visibility of institutions and pro-grams, the availability of community leaders, and local media.

270. Reid, Richard A., Betty J. Eberle, Lois Gonzales, Naomi L. Quenk, and Robert Oseasohn. "Rural Medical Care An Ex-perimental Delivery System." <u>American Journal of Public Health</u>, 65:266-271 (March, 1975).

> Describes the design and operation of an experimental delivery system which is providing medical care to families residing in Torrance County, New Mexico. Special attention is given to the components of the system and the characteristics and medical problems of its users.

271. Robinson, Ira E. See entry number 772.

272. Rosen, Catherine E., Sandra J. Coppage, Sandra J. Troglin, and Sidney Rosen. "Cost Effective Mental Health Services for the Rural Elderly." In Paul K. H. Kim and P. C. Wilson (eds.), <u>Toward Mental Health of the Rural Elderly</u>. Washingotn, D. C.: University Press of America, 1981. Pp. 165-186.

> Describes a program which provides preventive mental health services to the rural elderly. Presents the findings of an AoA study designed to evaluate the impact of the program upon the lives of the rural elderly. Interviews were used to assess social, psycho-logical, and physical functioning of members of thera-py groups and control groups.

273. Rosen, S., et. al. "Preventive Mental Health Services

for Rural Elderly." Paper presented at the Annual Meeting of the Gerontological Society of America (Dallas, Texas; 19-78).

274. Sebastian, Margaret. See entry number 11.

275. Shanas, Ethel. "Reported Illness and the Utilization of Medical Care." Public Welfare, 18:103-105 (April, 1960).

> Examines illness in the elderly and the importance of financial resources in the utilization of health care. Data are from a 1957 study of the Health Needs of Older People made by the National Opinion Research Center of the University of Chicago.

276. Sheps, Cecil G. See entry number 641.

277. Sias, John D., and Nancy J. Treat. "Health Care Delivery Systems to Rural, Aged, Disadvantaged - A Community Alternative." Paper presented at the 33rd Annual Meeting of the Gerontological Society of America (San Diego, California, November, 1980).

> A group of businessmen united to solve the problem of a lack of medical care in a rural county in Pennsylvania. Describes the creation of an organization providing a non-profit, tax exempt, community owned building leasing space to medically related service providers.

278. Smitson, Walter S. "Expanding Geriatric Services in a Rural State Hospital." Social Casework, 47:32-36 (January, 1966).

> A history, description, and evaluation of one state hospital's approach to improving its program for elderly patients and helping them find appropriate living accommodations when possible.

279. Stafford, Magdalen Marrow. See entry number 777.

280. Stoller, Eleanor Palo. See entry number 354.

281. Tancredi, Lawrence R. (ed.) "Ethics of Health Care." Paper presented at the Conference on Health Care and Changing Values (Washington, D. C.; November, 1973).

> Examines social-ethical problems of health care with special focus on the distribution of services and limited resources. Intended to be the basis for future research.

282. United States House, Select Committee on Aging, Subcommittee on Health and Long Term Care. Problems of Maine's rural elderly. (Hearing, 94th Congress, 2nd Session, March

27th.) Washington, D. C.: United States Government Printing Office, 1976.

283. United States House, Select Committee on Aging. Rural
elderly access to emergency medical services. (Hearing, 96-
1, May 7th; Committee Publication #96-198.) Washington, D.
C.: United States Government Printing Office, 1979.

284. United States House, Select Committee on Aging. Health
care for the rural elderly. (Hearing 96-1, 96th Congress,
1st Session; Publication #96-194, August 3rd.) Washington,
D. C.: United States Government Printing Office, 1979.

285. United States Senate, Committee on Agriculture and
Forestry. "Rural Health Care Delivery." Proceedings of a
National Conference on Rural Health Care Maintainance Organi-
cations (Washington, D. C.; October, 1974).

286. Washington, Becky. "Pooling Rural Resources." In
Perspective on Aging-Thirty Years 1950-1980. Washington,
D. C.: National Council on Aging, March/April, 1980. p. 6.

> Describes National Council on the Aging's supportive
> role to the Cherokee Nation's Geriatric Health Pro-
> gram which serves 14 rural northeastern Oklahoma
> counties.

287. Willie, C. V. "Health Care Needs of the Disadvantaged
in a Rural-Urban Area." HSMHA Health Reports, 87:81-86 (January, 1972).

> In upstate New York, 200 health professionals, agency
> executives, and community association leaders were
> contacted by mail and asked to identify health care
> needs of poor people, older people, and disadvantaged
> minority group members. The outstanding health care
> and service needs are described.

288. Ybarra, George. See entry number 792.

289. Ybarra, George, et. al. Comprehensive Care to the
Elderly: An Annotated Bibliography. Austin, Texas: Texas
University at Austin Center for Social Work Research, 1977.

> Provides some coverage of the rural elderly.

HOUSING AND LIVING ENVIRONMENT

290. Atchley, Robert C., and Sheila J. Miller. "Housing
and the Rural Aged." In Robert C. Atchley with Thomas O.
Byerts (eds.), Rural Environments and Aging. Washington, D.
C.: Gerontological Society, 1975. Pp. 95-143.

> A summary of what is known about the housing of the

rural elderly based on information from the 1970 census. Presents information on: types and sizes of households, characteristics of housing, indicies of housing adequacy, housing costs, and housing programs. Includes many tables.

291. Atchley, Robert C., and Sheila J. Miller. "Excerpt From 'Housing and the Rural Aged'." In Mildred M. Seltzer, Sherry L. Corbett, and Robert C. Atchley (eds.), Social Problems of the Aging. Belmont, California: Wadsworth Publishing Co., 1978.

292. Atchley, Robert C., and Sheila J. Miller. "Housing and Households of the Rural Aged." In Thomas O. Byerts, Sandra C. Howell, and Leon A. Pastalan (eds.), Environmental Context of Aging: Life-Styles, Environmental Quality, and Living Arrangements. New York, New York: Garland STPM Press, 1979. Pp. 62-79.

Using 1970 census data the authors explore the composition, characteristics, and adequacy of rural elderly households. Findings indicate that housing of the rural elderly is of poorer quality than urban elderly housing. Argues that federal support for housing programs for the rural aged has been limited.

293. Beall, George T., Marie M. Thompson, F. Godwin, and W. T. Donahue. Housing Older Persons in Rural America: A Handbook on Congregate Housing. Washington, D. C.: International Center for Social Gerontology, 1981.

Provides an overview and technical guidance on the process of planning and providing congregate housing to the rural elderly. Contains sections on: background, generating community interest, preliminary planning, financing construction, design, management, and supportive services.

294. Britton, J. H. "Living in a Rural Pennsylvania Community in Old Age." In F. M. Carp (ed.), Patterns of Living and Housing of Middle Aged and Older People. Public Health Service, Publication #1496, 1965.

295. Buckholz, Marjorie. See entry number 520.

296. Bylund, Robert A. See entry number 726.

297. Bylund, Robert A. See entry number 727.

29{ Bylund, Robert A. See entry number 728.

299. Cowles, May L. "Housing and Associated Problems of the Rural Farm Aged Population in Two Wisconsin Counties." Rural Sociology, 21:239-249 (September-December, 1956).

Based on interviews with 429 persons, this study pre-

sents information on the problems facing the rural-
farm aged. Major housing problems identified include:
lack of modern heating and plumbing facilities, dan-
gerous stairs, and lack of money to improve housing
quality. The author observes that these housing needs
do not differ much from those of other elderly in-
dviduals.

300. Derr, Don A., and Nelson L. LeRay. "Housing in the
Nonmetropolitan Northeast: Differences Among Growing, Sta-
ble and Declining Areas." Bulletin #487. Washington, D. C.:
Northeast Regional Community Services in Cooperation with
Economic Development Division, United States Department of
Agriculture, n.d.

301. Donnenwerth, Gregory U. See entry number 379.

302. Edwards, J. N. See entry number 443.

303. Gish, Pat B. See entry number 74.

304. Horn, M. J., et. al. Housing for the Elderly. Springfield, Virginia: National Technical Information Service,
Department of Commerce, 1973.

　　　　Presents data from 100 low-income rural households
　　　　headed by the elderly.

305. Hussey, H. M. Housing for the Elderly - A Conceptual
Framework. Springfield, Virginia: National Technical Information Service, United States Department of Commerce, 1973.

　　　　This study describes the housing and housing satisfac-
　　　　tion of 100 rural Nevada families headed by elderly
　　　　persons.

306. Kim, Paul K. H. See entry number 151.

307. Larson, Donald K. See entry number 456.

308. Lawton, M. Powell. How the Elderly Live. Washington,
D. C.: Gerontological Society, 1971.

　　　　Discusses how the elderly adapt to different living
　　　　environments such as the inner city, institutions,
　　　　and rural areas.

309. Lawton, M. Powell. See entry number 684.

310. Montgomery, James E. "Housing of the Rural Aged." In
E. Grant Youmans (ed.), Older Rural Americans. Lexington,
Kentucky: University of Kentucky Press, 1967. Pp. 169-194.

　　　　A general discussion of housing conditions and needs
　　　　of the rural elderly using 1960 Census statistics.

Focuses on home ownership, housing satisfaction, home improvements, home location, and policies and programs aimed at improving rural housing.

311. Montgomery, James E., Alice C. Stubbs, and Savannah S. Day. "The Housing Environment of the Rural Elderly." The Gerontologist, 20:444-451 (1980).

Using data from personal interviews with 273 older couples and 298 older women living alone in 17 rural, low-income southern counties, this study examines housing characteristics and conditions, housing perceptions, and steps taken to improve dwellings. Most respondents indicated their housing was adequate but also cited the need for improvement in small ways.

312. Nahemow, Lucille. See entry number 766.

313. Nathanson, Iric. Housing needs of the rural elderly and handicapped. Department of Housing and Urban Development Office of Policy Development and Research, 1980.

314. Noll, P. F. Federally Assisted Housing Programs for the Elderly in Rural Areas - Programs and Prospects. Washington, D. C.: Housing Assistance Council, Inc., August, 1978.

315. Parenti, F. R. Provision of Housing for the Rural Elderly Under Major Federal Housing Programs. Washington, D. C.: United States Senate Subcommittee on Rural Development, 1976.

316. Powers, R. C., et. al. "Needs and opportunities for the rural elderly to continue independent living." Ames, Iowa: Iowa State University, 1977.

This monograph examines the factors that facilitate independent living among the elderly of rural Iowa.

317. Rowles, Graham D. "Growing Old 'Inside': Aging and Attachment to Place in an Appalachian Community." In Nancy Datan and Nancy Lohmann (eds.), Transitions of Aging. New York, New York: Academic Press, 1980. Pp. 153-170.

This paper explores several aspects of the place attachment found among 15 elderly residents of a very small Appalachian community. The discussion focuses on the importance of the elderly's familiarity of their surroundings.

318. Rowles, Graham D. "The geographical experience of the elderly: final progress report." A final report to the National Institute on Aging, August, 1981.

The final report of the author's three year participant

observation study of 15 elderly Appalachian residents.
The major purpose of the research was to explore how
the elderly experience and interact with their geographical environment.

319. Rowles, Graham D. "Spatial Dimensions of Social Support in Rural Appalachia." Paper presented at the 34th Annual Meeting of the Gerontological Society of America (Toronto,
Canada; November, 1981).

Explores the spatial and environmental dimensions of
social support with data from a three year participant
observation study of a panel of elderly persons in a
rural Appalachian community. Identifies a hierarchy
of spaces from which different forms and intensities
of support are derived. These spaces are: home,
surveillance zone, vicinity, community, sub-region,
region, and nation.

320. Rowles, Graham D. "The Surveillance Zone as Meaning-
ful Space for the Aged." The Gerontologist, 21(3):304-311
(1981).

Another article reporting on the way in which rural
Appalachian elderly experience their geographical
environment. This paper develops and examines the
concept of the "surveillance zone" - the outside
area that can be observed from inside the home. The
watching of this zone plays important supportive and
integrative functions for the elderly.

321. Rowles, Graham D. "Between Worlds: A Relocation Dilemma for the Appalachian Elderly." International Journal
of Aging and Human Development (in press), 1983.

322. Rowles, Graham D. "Aging in Rural Environments." In
I. Altman, J. Wohlwill and M. P. Lawton (eds.), Environments
for the Elderly. New York, New York: Plenum Press (in
press), 1983.

323. Sanoff, Henry. "An Architectural Researcher's Reaction
to the Papers." In Robert C. Atchley with Thomas O. Byerts
(eds.), Rural Environments and Aging. Washington, D. C.:
Gerontological Society, 1975. Pp. 223-227.

Discusses the problems of the rural elderly and what
housing design can and cannot do to alleviate those
problems.

324. Schooler, Kermit K. See entry number 218.

325. Sherman, S. "Satisfaction With Retirement Housing."
Aging and Human Development, 3(4) (November):339-366.

326. United States House, Committee on Government Operations.
Housing for the elderly: the federal response. (94th Con-

gress, lst Session, Report 94-376; House Reports 3-4:13101-13104.) Washington, D. C.: United States Government Printing Office, 1975.

327. United States House, Select Committee on Aging, Subcommittee on Housing and Consumer Interests. Oversight Hearing on Action 202. (94th Congress, 2nd Session, September, 10th.) Washington, D. C.: United States Government Printing Office, 1976.

328. United States House, Select Committee on Aging. Urban and rural housing for the elderly. (Hearing, Jamestown, New York, August 17th.) Washington, D. C.: United States Government Printing Office, 1974.

329. United States Senate, Subcommittee on Housing and Urban Affairs. Oversight on rural housing programs. (Hearings, November 19th - 21st.) Washington, D. C.: United States Government Printing Office, 1974.

330. Wilkinson, Carroll Wetzel. See entry number 178.

331. Wilkinson, Carroll Wetzel. See entry number 179.

332. Windley, Paul G. "The Effects of the Ecological/Architectural Dimensions of Small Rural Towns on the Well-being of Older People." In Paul K. H. Kim and C. P. Wilson (eds.), Toward Mental Health of the Rural Elderly. Washington, D. C.: University Press of America, 1981. Pp. 81-96.

   Describes a study of 990 residents of 18 small towns
   ranging in population from 105 to 2,500. Focuses on
   the relationship of the elderly's mental health and
   the psychosocial and ecological/architectural characteristics of their environments.

333. Windley, Paul G. See entry number 202.

334. Windley, Paul G. See entry number 675.

335. Woolrich, A. M., et. al. "Housing requirements of the elderly." Fort Collins, Colorado: Colorado State University, 1975.

336. Yenerall, Joseph D. "Some Social Dimensions of Variations in Housing Type for the Elderly in Communities in St. Lawrence County, New York." Paper presented at the 19th Annual Meeting of the New York State Sociological Association, Alfred University, Alfred, New York (October, 1971).

INFORMAL SUPPORT NETWORKS

337. Bourg, Carroll J. "Differentiation, Centrality, and Solidarity in Rural Environments: Remarks, Analysis, and

Reflections." In Robert C. Atchley with Thomas O. Byerts
(eds.), Rural Environments and Aging. Washington, D. C.:
Gerontological Society, 1975. Pp. 235-237.

> A summary and conclusion chapter. Includes concluding
> remarks, analysis of the papers, and reflections of
> emerging issues.

338. Coward, Raymond T. "The Other Side of the Coin: Cau-
tions About the Role of Natural Helping Networks in Programs
for the Rural Elderly." In N. Stinnett (ed.), Building Family Strengths - Volume 4. Lincoln, Nebraska: The University
of Nebraska Press (in press), 1983.

339. Deimling, Gary T., and Lynn W. Huber. "The Availability and Participation of Immediate Kin in Caring for Rural
Elderly." Paper presented at the Annual Meeting of the Gerontological Society of America (Toronto, Canada; November,
1981).

> Based on preliminary reports on a family caregiving
> study of 647 families from a range of geographic lo-
> cations from inner city to rural farm. Presents an
> overview of similarities and differences between care-
> giving patterns of urban and rural families. Differ-
> ences found are minimal.

340. Douglas, Barbara. "Relationships Among Coping Styles,
Personal Contact Networks, and Selected Demographics Among
Rural Elderly Women." Paper presented at the Annual Meeting
of the Gerontological Society of America (Toronto, Canada;
November, 1981).

> Reports data from a study of psychological and sub-
> cultural variation among a sample of 122 noninstitu-
> tionalized elderly females living in four rural Oregon
> towns. Contacts and coping styles were found to vary
> between towns. Coping styles were also found to be
> different from younger populations while contact pat-
> terns were unlike those attributed to urban culture.

341. Ehrlich, Phyllis Diane. "Exploratory study of infor-
mal support systems in meeting health needs of elderly per-
sons in a rural area." (Doctoral dissertation, Southern
Illinois University at Carbondale, Carbondale, Illinois,
August, 1982.) Dissertation Abstracts International, 43, 2,
A, p.548.

> This study examines the relationship between community
> based informal support networks and the rural elderly's
> ability to perform activities of daily living. Inter-
> views with 80 noninstitutionalized elderly were used
> to collect data on the respondents health, nature of
> informal support systems, and resource environment. No
> consistent relationship was found between functional
> health and network functionality.

342. Ehrlich, Phyllis Diane. "Informal Support Networks and Functional Health of Rural Elderly." Paper presented at the 35th Annual Meeting of the Gerontological Society of America (Boston, Massachusetts; November, 1982).

> Explores the relationships among three dimensions: health, informal networks, and services. Half of the 80 respondents were from towns with centralized services and half from towns with more dispersed services. The findings appear to match those found for the urban elderly quite closely.

343. Goudy, Willis J. See entry number 382.

344. Heltsley, Mary E., and Ronald C. Powers. "Social Interaction and Perceived Adequacy of Interaction of the Rural Aged." The Gerontologist, 15(6):533-536 (December, 1975).

> Uses data from 1971 interviews of residents of small southwestern Iowa towns to discuss differences among rural elderly in frequency of social contact and the perceived adequacy of that contact. Major findings are; health status is unrelated to interaction, closer proximity is associated with more interaction, and parents did not necessarily find interaction with children satisfying.

345. Hooyman, Nancy R., and N. Scott. "A Mutual Help Model for Rural Elderly Women." The Gerontologist, 19:91(1979).

> An examination of the special problems of rural aged females and a discussion of the need for mutual support networks to help in dealing with these problems. The authors argue that the exchange inherent in such networks meshes with rural values and that help organizations will increase social participation and help meet needs.

346. Hooyman, Nancy R. "Mutual Help Organizations For Rural Older Women." Educational Gerontology, 5(4):429-447 (1980).

> Describes some of the problems and needs of rural older women. Suggests that mutual help organizations can meet some of those needs. Stresses common problem solving and reciprocity of help as most important elements of this kind of support network. Functions and educational implications are outlined.

347. Krout, John A. "Bridging the Gap: Informal and Formal Supports of the Rural Elderly." Symposium presentation at the Annual Meeting of the Gerontological Society of America (Boston, Massachusetts; November, 1982).

> Examines the roles that informal networks play in the provision of assistance to the elderly living in rural settings. Special attention is played to the strengths

and weaknesses of such networks and in the kinds of linkages with formal supports that could improve their functioning.

348. Nowak, Carol A. "Informal Networks of Support in Later Life: Conceptual Methodological, and Applied Rural vs. Urban Issues." Paper presented at the Annual Meeting of the National Conference on Aging (Washington, D. C.; April, 1982).

Looks into the question of rural/urban differences in the area of informal network support of the elderly. Covers topics such as kin proximity in later life, site of later life caregiving, assessment of caregiver needs, and the role of non-kin in later life need satisfaction.

349. Patterson, S. L. "A Study of the Mutuality Relationship Among Older Rural Natural Helpers." Paper presented at the 35th Annual Meeting of the Gerontological Society of America (Boston, Massachusetts; November, 1982).

Examines the nature of the relationships between older rural natural helpers. Five related dimensions found to characterize mutuality relationships are identified and examined: motivation, commonality of experience, availability, outreach, and role reversibility.

350. Powers, Edward A., et. al. "The role of confidants in friendship patterns of older persons." Ames, Iowa: Iowa State University, Department of Sociology and Anthropology, 1974.

This study examines the relationships between elderly persons and their "confidants" for a sample of over 200 persons living in five rural and urban Iowa counties. Half of the elderly reported having such a relationship.

351. Scott, Jean Pearson. See entry number 401.

352. Stafford, Magdalen Marrow. See entry number 777.

353. Steele, G. Alec. See entry number 474.

354. Stoller, Eleanor Palo. "Growing Older in the Country: The Role of Informal Support Networks." Paper presented at the Annual Meeting of the Rural Sociological Society (Burington, Vermont; August, 1979).

Examines the contribution of informal support networks in the long-term care of the rural elderly. Discusses the advantages of developing informal networks from the economic and social psychological point of view.

355. Taietz, Philip. See entry number 151.

356. Yang, Yue-Eng. "Natural support systems and the rural
elderly: a Missouri case." (Doctoral dissertation, Cultural Anthropology, University of Missouri, Columbia, Missouri,
1979.) Dissertation Abstracts International, 40, 9, A, p.
5105.

> An ethnographic case study of the elderly's utiliza-
> tion of supportive services in a small central Missouri
> farming community. Informal supports (family, rela-
> tives, friends) were found to be the most important
> source of support in many areas such as emotional and
> task performance. Formal service programs were gen-
> erally not relied upon because of the elderly's lack
> of knowledge or distrust of them.

LEISURE AND RECREATION

357. Bley, N. D. See entry number 1.

358. Cozart, E. S., and M. C. Evashwich. "Developing a
Recreational Program for Patients in a Rural Nursing Home."
Public Health Report, 93:369-374 (1978).

> This short article describes the development of a
> recreational program for rural elderly nursing home
> patients.

359. Frekany, G. A., and D. K. Leslie. "Developing an Ex-
ercise Program for Senior Citizens." Therapeutic Recreation
Journal, 8:178-189 (1974).

> A brief description of an elderly exercise program
> initiated in several rural Iowa counties. The program
> was found to have a positive effect on participant's
> physical and social well-being.

360. Gullie, R. "Cohoes Elderly Swim Their Way to Fitness."
New York State Recreation and Park Society Journal, 1:8-10
(1978).

> Describes a swimming exercise program found in a small
> New York community.

361. Hoar, I. "A Study of Free-Time Activities of 200 Aged
Persons." Sociology and Social Research, 45(2):157-163 (19-
61).

> An examination of the leisure-time activities of 200
> rural Mississippi elderly. The author says that in-
> creased amounts of and changes in recreational activi-
> ties were beneficial for the elderly. Leisure time
> differences for males and females are discussed.

362. Kim, Paul K. H. See entry number 151.

363. Kivett, Vira R., and Dennis Orthner. "Activity Patterns and Leisure Preferences of Rural Elderly with Visual
Impairment." Therapeutic Recreation Journal, 14(2):49-58
(1980).

This paper reports on the findings from an analysis
of data collected from a group of 236 visually impaired rural aged drawn from a larger study. These
visually impaired elderly when compared to the non-
impaired reported: greater dependence on others for
transportation, less participation in group activities,
less visits with friends and neighbors, and higher
levels of loneliness. The authors present recommeda-
tions on the planning of leisure services to the visually impaired rural elderly.

364. Leitner, Michael J., et. al. "Recreation and the
rural elderly." College Park, Maryland: Center on Aging,
University of Maryland, 1980.

A literature review on recreation for the rural elderly consisting of seven sections including a summary
section and an annotated bibliography with 83 citations. The sections are as follows: rural elderly
needs, leisure activities, existing recreation programs, provision of services, meeting the rural elderly's recreational needs, and conclusions and recommendations.

365. Lowe, Laura Gertrude. See entry number 111.

366. McIntoch, William Alex, and Peggy A. Shifflett. "Veg-
etable Gardening as Leisure or as Dietary Supplement: A
Preliminary Investigation." Paper presented at the Annual
Meeting of the Rural Sociological Society (San Francisco,
California; September, 1982).

Examines vegetable gardening habits of the rural elderly with data from a study conducted for the U. S. Department of Agriculture in the Central Shenandoah Planning District, Virginia. Nearly 70% of the sample reported gardening with the intensity of gardening related to sociodemographic, socioeconomic and mass media
exposure variables.

367. McKain, Walter C., Jr. "Community Roles and Activities
of Older Rural Persons." In E. Grant Youmans (ed.), Older
Rural Americans. Lexington, Kentucky: University of Kentucky Press, 1967. Pp. 75-96.

General essay with much literature review on community
roles of rural elderly. Examines use of free time,
formal and informal social participation, and community
involvement and service.

368. Mancini, Jay A. "Discretionary Time Use Among Older Adults in Rural Areas: Implications for Practitioners." Paper presented at the Annual Meeting of the Southern Gerontological Society (Atlanta, Georgia; 1981).

369. Weller, Margaret Ann. "Services supportive to leisure pursuits of selected rural elderly." (Doctoral dissertation, Indiana University, Bloomington, Indiana, February, 1980.) Dissertation Abstracts International, 41, 8, A, p.3821.

> A study of the resources available in two Indiana rural counties for the support of the aged's leisure experiences. Data was collected form both agencies and 197 rural elderly respondents. Few of the agencies were found to have programs specifically designed for the elderly nor were the elderly generally aware of those services or leisure experiences available.

370. Wilkinson, Carroll Wetzel. See entry number 178.

371. Wilkinson, Carroll Wetzel. See entry number 179.

372. Youmans, E. Grant. See entry number 795.

LIFE SATISFACTION AND MORALE

373. Baines, Elizabeth Murrow. "An investigation of life satisfaction in the nursing home resident in selected rural midwest communities." (Doctoral dissertation, University of Nebraska, Lincoln, Nebraska, November, 1981.) Dissertation Abstracts International, 42, 5, A, P.2321.

> This study examines the relationship between life satisfaction and type of nursing home (profit or nonprofit). A total sample of 200 elderly nursing home residents were drawn from the populations of two nonprofit and three proprietary homes located in rural midwest cities. Ninety percent of the respondents indicated satisfaction with their lives with little differences found between nursing home types.

374. Blake, Brian F., and Joseph F. Donnemeyer. "Age and Orientations Toward Rural Community Environments." Paper presented at the Annual Meeting of the Rural Sociological Society (Burlington, Vermont; August, 1979).

> Reports data from a survey of 3,451 residents of Indiana designed to determine what they feel their community can offer for their subjective well being. Also examines the degree to which these perceptions are comparable among elderly and younger rural and urban residents.

375. Britton, J. H., and W. G. Mather. "Personal and Social

Adjustment of Rural Older Persons." Journal of Gerontology, 12:436 (1957).

> Examines expectations of a rural Pennsylvania community for its older people, variables in their adjustment, and methods of assessing their personal and social adequacy.

376. Curry, T. J., et. al. "Nursing Home Size vs. Life Satisfaction." The Gerontologist, 13:295-298 (Autumn, 1973).

> This study, conducted in rural Ohio, focuses on the relationship between nursing home size and life satisfaction. No significant association between these variables was found.

377. DeShane, Michael Robert. See entry number 733.

378. Danforth, Diana M., Mary Jo Grindstead-Schneider, and Donald E. Voth. "Self-Perceived Health and Life Outlook Among the Rural Elderly." Paper presented at the Annual Meeting of the Rural Sociological Society (Burlington, Vermont; August, 1979).

> Examines differences in life outlook and self-perceived health among 495 elderly people from two rural counties in western Arkansas. The old-old saw their health more positively than the young-old and had lower levels of life satisfaction. Education was the strongest predictor of self-perceived health.

379. Donnenwerth, Gregory V., Rebecca F. Guy, and Melissa J. Norvell. "Life Satisfaction Among Older Persons: Rural-Urban and Racial Comparisons." Social Science Quarterly, 59:578-583 (December, 1978).

> Investigates the effect of residence and race on life satisfaction of older persons in western Tennessee. Also examines the effects of age, income, and frequency of social contacts. Findings indicate rural dwellers and whites have higher levels of life satisfaction. The authors, however, stress the importance of the interactions between the other three independent variables in interpreting these findings.

380. Ergood, Bruce, and Robert K. Shelly. "Correlates of life satisfaction in a rural elderly population." Athens, Ohio: Ohio University, 1979.

381. Goudy, Willis J. "Evaluations of Local Attributes and Community Satisfaction in Small Towns." Rural Sociology, 42:371-382 (1977).

> Data are from mailed questionnaires returned by 4,627 individuals from north-central Iowa. Perceptions of local attributes such as citizen participation and

commitment to the community are hypothesized to be
more efficient predictors of community satisfaction
than are perceptions of services.

382. Goudy, Willis J. "Local Social Ties and Life Satisfaction of Older People in Selected Iowa Communities." Paper presented at the Annual Meeting of the Rural Sociological
Society (Guelph, Ontario; August, 1981).

Examines the relationships between family and friendship ties, community involvement, and quality of life
for 2,451 older residents of 27 towns in six counties
in north central Iowa. The findings showed consider-
ble variation between communities and general conclusions could not be drawn.

383. Heltsley, M. E. "Patterns of living of the rural aged:
satisfactions, preferences and choices." Ames, Iowa: Iowa
State University, 1974.

384. Hynson, Lawrence M., Jr.   See entry number 742.

385. Hynson, Lawrence M., Jr.   See entry number 743.

386. Jolley, J. "Alienation and Depression in the Small
Town Widow." Paper presented at the Annual Meeting of the
Gerontological Society of America (Toronto, Canada; November,
1981).

Investigates the relationship of alienation and depression to social interaction in 61 small town widows
and married women. The widows were found to be significantly more alienated and depressed. The implications of these findings for existing research are
discussed.

387. Kim, Paul K. H.   See entry number 151.

388. Kinard, J. D., and Vira R. Kivett. "Morale and Mealtime Companionship in the Rural Elderly." Paper presented
at the 35th Annual Meeting of the Gerontological Society
of America (Boston, Massachusetts; November, 1982).

Examines the relationship between social interaction
at mealtime and nutritional status and morale with data
from 418 rural people aged 65 or older. The use of
control variables in a multiple regression analysis
resulted in a finding of no relationship between mealtime companionship and morale.

389. Kivett, Vira R. "Loneliness and the Rural Black Elderly: Perspectives on Intervention." Black Aging, 3:160-166
(1978).

An analysis of the level of loneliness among a sample

of 135 rural black elderly. Several variables were found to be positively associated with loneliness including inadequate transportation, loss of spouse, and poor eye sight.

390. Kivett, Vira R. "Discriminators of Loneliness Among the Rural Elderly: Implications for Intervention." The Gerontologist, 19(1):108-115 (1979).

Uses stepwise discriminant analysis to determine the most important discriminators of loneliness among a sample of 419 rural elderly. Adequacy of transportation, frequency of telephoning, self-rated health, widowhood, organizational activity, single adulthood, and adequacy of eyesight are the most important classifiers.

391. Kivett, Vira R. See entry number 418.

392. Kivett, Vira R., and R. Max Learner. "Situational Influences on the Morale of Older Rural Adults in Child-Shared Housing: A Comparative Analysis." The Gerontologist, 22: 100-106 (February, 1982).

A study of the impact of housing arrangements on the subjective well-being of rural adults. No significant difference was found in the morale scores of those elderly living with children versus other arrangements when controlling for health.

393. Kushman, John E. See entry number 454.

394. Lee, Gary R. See entry number 754.

395. McKain, Walter C., Jr. See entry number 761.

396. Miller, Michael K. See entry number 764.

397. Pihlblad, C. Terence, R. Hessler, and H. Freshley. The Rural Elderly, 8 Years Later: Changes in Life Satisfaction, Living Arrangements, and Health Status. Washington, D. C.: Administration on Aging, Grant #93-P-57673, 1976.

Describes the results of a 1973-74 follow up survey of 568 rural Missouri elderly originally interviewed in 1966. Participation in formal social activities was reported to be low, especially for elderly men.

398. Pihlblad, C. Terence, and Robert L. McNamara. "Social Adjustment of Elderly People in Three Small Towns." In Arnold M. Rose, and Warren A. Peterson (eds.), Older People and Their Social World. Philadelphia, Pennsylvania: F. A. Davis Co., 1965. Pp. 49-73.

Using a modification of a scale developed by Hairghurst

and Cavan, this study examines the social adjustment
of elderly residents of central Missouri. In-home
interviews were conducted in two small villages and
a larger town of about 7,000 population. Social adjustment was found to be greatest for those who had:
good health, higher income, higher levels of social
participation, and were married.

399. Sauer, William J. See entry number 774.

400. Scott, Jean Pearson. "Single Rural Elders: A Comparison of Dimensions of Life Satisfaction." Alternative
Life Styles, 2(3): (August, 1979).

    A comparison of 30 individuals who remained single
    throughout their lives with 214 married and 163 widow-
    ed elderly. While the groups did not differ on life
    satisfaction in general, single persons reported
    greater loneliness and unhappiness.

401. Scott, Jean Pearson. "The Influences of Family and
Friend Relationships on Subjective Well-Being: A Multivari-
ate Study of the Rural Elderly." Paper presented at the
Annual Meeting of the Southern Gerontological Society (Atlanta, Georgia, 1981).

402. Scott, Taylor Carver. "A pattern of adjustment of an
aged rural population in New Windsor, Maryland." (Doctoral
dissertation, University of Maryland, College Park, Maryland,
1967.) Dissertation Abstracts International, 28, 9, A,
p.3782.

    This dissertation examines data on the adjustment pat-
    terns of 123 elderly persons living in a rural Mary-
    land community. The primary purpose of the study was
    to evaluate the validity of disengagement theory ver-
    sus other conceptualizations of successful adjustment
    among the elderly. Good adjustment among the elderly
    was found to be associated with active participation
    and a maintenance of roles established earlier in life.

403. Stojanovic, Elisabeth J. "Morale and its correlates
among aged black and white rural women in Mississippi."
(Doctoral dissertation, Lousiana State University and Agricultural and Mining College, April, 1970.) Dissertation
Abstracts International, 31, 10, A, p.5540.

    A study of morale of elderly black and white low in-
    come rural Mississippi women using a panel study de-
    sign. Data was collected in 1961 and again in 1966.
    The major finding is that morale among aged rural
    women was associated with self-image and activity
    patterns. Differences between white and black elderly
    women are discussed.

404. Windley, Paul G., and Rick J. Scheidt. "The Well-Being of Older Persons in Small Rural Towns: A Town Panel Approach." Educational Gerontology, 5(4):355-373 (October, 1970).

> An interdisciplinary study of older residents of small rural towns. Nearly 1,000 interviews from 18 small towns in Kansas were conducted to assess residents' well-being, assess perceptions of their environment, and to determine the extent to which well-being can be predicted by environmental features. A large amount of variation was found in the levels of well-being and satisfaction for residents of the different communities.

405. Youmans, E. Grant. See entry number 802.

406. Youmans, E. Grant. See entry number 796.

MINORITIES

407. Arling, Greg. See entry number 854.

408. Bastida, Elena. "The Rural Minority Elderly: In Greater Isolation and Need." Paper presented at the Annual Meeting of the Gerontological Society of America (San Diego, California; November, 1980).

> Compares samples of the minority elderly from a midwestern metropolitan area and two rural settings in the same region (total n=300). The rural minority elderly are found to be poorer and in greater need of community services. Planning and policy making recommendations are also presented.

409. Christopherson, Victor A. See entry number 63.

410. Coyle, J. M., and K. S. Lanham. "Life Situations of the Rural Black Elderly in Louisiana." Paper presented at the Annual Meeting of the Gerontological Society of America (San Diego, California; November, 1980).

> Reports the results of a 1979 pilot study investigating the status and needs of the black elderly in a rural area. Most subjects were rated as being moderately impaired on items such as economic resources physical and mental health, and social activities.

411. Davis, Katherine Conway. See entry number 19.

412. Decker, James T. "Native American Family Practice: The Role of Grandparents in Social Programs." Generations, (Western Gerontological Society), Fall:15 (1977).

> A very brief discussion of a program designed to in-

volve older native Americans in family advocate programs.

413. Donnenwerth, Gregory V. See entry number 379.

414. Goldenrod Hills Community Action Council. See entry
number 496.

415. Gordon, Jacob U. See entry number 547.

416. Jeffries, Willie. Our Aged Indians: Triple Jeopardy-
Myth or Reality? Washington, D. C.: National Council on
the Aging, Inc., (April) 1972. Pp. 7-10.

417. Kivett, Vira R. See entry number 389.

418. Kivett, Vira R. "The Importance of Race to the Life
of the Rural Elderly." Paper presented at the Annual Meeting of the Gerontological Society of America (Toronto, Canada; November, 1981).

Examines the relative importance of race in differentiating a sample of 418 older rural adults on a number
of quality of life factors. Race was found to be important only in regards to three variables: income
adequacy, life satisfaction, and decision to live with
a daughter or son. Author concludes that health,
social, and economic factors are more important than
race as determinants of quality of life among the elderly studied.

419. Lanham, Karen, and Jean M. Coyle. "A Needs-Assessment
Survey of Black Rural Elderly Persons in Northeast Louisiana:
Issues and Impressions." Paper presented at the Southwest-
ern Sociological Association (Houston, Texas; April, 1980).

This paper presents data collected from a sample of
50 black elderly residents of a Louisiana county. A
detailed discussion of methodological problems encoun-
tered in the study is included.

420. Leonard, Olen E. "The Older Rural Spanish Speaking
People of the Southwest." In E. Grant Youmans (ed.), Older
Rural Americans. Lexington, Kentucky: University of Ken-
tucky Press, 1967. Pp. 239-261.

Discusses older rural Spanish people residing in the
southwest. Examines social, economic, and health
status and family and community roles using 1960
census data. Problems of adjustment and economic and
social trends are also examined.

421. Levy, Jerrold E. "The Older American Indian." In E.
Grant Youmans (ed.), Older Rural Americans. Lexington, Kentucky: University of Kentucky Press, 1967. Pp. 221-238.

Defines the Indian population, notes relevant differences in cultures and values, and discusses present
needs of the elderly American Indian. Focuses on the
Blackfoot and Navajo.

422. McConatha, Douglas. See entry number 597.

423. National Center on the Black Aged. Manpower Needs of
the Rural Black Elderly. Washington, D. C., 1975.

424. National Center on the Black Aged. Technical Bulletin,
Washington, D. C., June, 1975.

Examines the problems of the rural black elderly.

425. Paringer, Lyn. See entry number 215.

426. Rosen, Catherine E. "A Comparison of Black and White
Rural Elderly." Paper presented at the 30th Annual Meeting
of the Gerontological Society of America (San Francisco, California; November, 1977).

Compares black and white rural elderly with data collected from interviews with 694 Georgia residents.
The health and living conditions of blacks were found
to be significantly lower than those of whites. Whites,
however, had significantly fewer social resources.
Whereas blacks turned to family and social agencies
in times of need, whites turned to family or no one.
Implications for needs and services are discussed.

427. Smith, Stanley H. "The Older Rural Negro." In E.
Grant Youmans (eds.), Older Rural Americans. Lexington, Kentucky: University of Kentucky Press, 1967. Pp. 262-280.

Uses 1960 Census data to outline the demographic
characteristics of older rural blacks. Discusses
education, employment, income, involvement in American
life, and assesses their subjective well-being.

428. Spencer, Mary Emilie Sours. "The general well-being
of rural black elderly: a descriptive study." (Doctoral
dissertation, Sociology, Individual and Family Studies,
University of Maryland, College Park, Maryland, 1979.) Dissertation Abstracts International, 40, 6, A, p.3562.

A study of the status of a sample of 60 black elderly
living in a Maryland county. Data was analyzed on the
basis of sex and marital status and covers physical
health, mental health, social functioning, activities
of daily living, economic resources, and utilization
of formal services.

429. Stojanovic, Elisabeth J. See entry number 403.

430. Tucker, Charles Jackson. See entry number 38.

431. Washington, Becky. See entry number 286.

432. Watson, Wilbur. "Older Frail Rural Blacks: A Concept-
ualization and Analysis." National Center on Black Aged:
Quarterly Contact, 3(4):1-2 (1980).

   Reports data on levels of frailty for over 1,500 elderly rural southern black and whites.

433. Wilkinson, Carroll Wetzel. See entry number 179.

434. Willie, C. V. See entry number 287.

NEEDS AND PROBLEMS

435. Bastida, Elena. See entry number 408.

436. Bertrand, A. L. "Characteristics and problems of rural
aged in Louisiana." Baton Rouge, Louisiana: Louisiana State
University, Department of Rural Sociology, 1975.

437. Bertrand, A. L. The Aged in a Diffused Rural Society.
Springfield, Virginia: National Technical Information Service, United States Department of Commerce, 1973.

   A general discussion of the rural elderly and
   their problems. Applications for community program
   planning.

438. Bultena, G. L., et. al. "Life after seventy in Iowa:
A restudy of the aged." Sociology Report #95. Ames, Iowa:
Iowa State University, Department of Sociology, 1971.

   A restudy of over 200 rural and urban Iowa elderly
   initially interviewed in 1960. Covers a number of topics such as housing, ecomomic status, morale, and
   health problems.

439. Bylund, Robert, Charles O. Crawford, Nelson L. LeRay,
and Elinor M. Caravella. "The Rural Elderly in the United
States and the Northeast: A Statistical Report." Paper
presented at a workshop on Rural Gerontology Research in the
Northeast at the Northeast Regional Center for Rural Development, Cornell University, Department of Sociology, 1971.

   Defines the rural elderly population and stresses the
   need for research on their problems, needs, and wants.

440. Division of Research and Evaluation, Office of Research,
Demonstration and Evaluation. First Report on Needs and
Service Programs for the Rural Elderly. Washington, D. C.:
Administration on Aging, 1981.

441. Cowles, May L. See entry number 299.

442. Edwards, J. N. "Needs of aged in rural Virginia, 1973-1974." Blacksburg, Virginia: Virginia Polytechnical Institute, Department of Sociology, 1974.

443. Edwards, J. N., and D. L. Klemmack. "Perceived health, housing, and participation needs of the aged in rural Virginia." VPI Research Work Unit/Project Abstract VA-0616192. Blacksburg, Virginia: University of Virginia, Department of Sociology, 1980.

     Describes a study done in southwestern Virginia which
     examines quality of rural life and health, housing,
     and social needs.

444. Grams, Armin, and Alfred P. Fengler. "Vermont Elders: No Sense of Deprivation." Perspective on Aging, 10(1):12-15 (1981).

     This short paper presents an overview of the findings
     generated by a needs assessment survey of a sample of
     1,400 elderly living in four rural Vermont counties.
     The researchers report being struck by the discrepancy
     between objective evidence that the rural elderly have
     considerable needs and the elderly's own pronouncements
     indicating high levels of satisfaction.

445. Gunter, Patricia Lee. "A survey of the needs of the rural elderly in selected counties in southern Illinois." (Doctoral dissertation, Southern Illinois University at Carbondale, Illinois, 1980.) Dissertation Abstracts International, 41, 12, A, p.5261.

     Reports findings from a study of the status of a sample
     of 655 elderly living in 13 rural southern Illinois
     counties and of the services available to them from
     125 social services providers. The data show a gap
     between the elderly's self-perceptions and the service
     provider's perceptions of them.

446. Harbert, Anita S., and Carroll W. Wilkinson. "Growing Old in Rural America." Aging, 291-292:36-40 (January-February, 1979).

     Discusses problems and strengths of rural life for the
     elderly. Significant problems identified are: large
     distances from necessities and services, low income,
     inadequate housing, health problems, and knowledge of
     and attitudes towards services. Strengths include
     self-reliance and supportive social systems.

447. Harootyan, Robert. "Problems Facing the Rural Elderly: A Demographic View." Generations (Western Gerontological Society), 2(3):5-6 (Fall, 1977).

Discusses a number of indicators of need that show the
rural elderly to be worse off than their urban counterparts. Also argues that the distribution of elderly
within rural areas (they are over-represented in places
of 1,000 - 2,500 and under represented in outlying
areas) calls for a special policy response.

448. Kim, Paul K. H. See entry number 151.

449. Kivett, Vira R. "The Aged in North Carolina: Physical, Social, and Environmental Characteristics and Sources
of Assistance." The Guilford Study. Raleigh, North Carolina: North Carolina State University, North Carolina Agricultural Experiment Station, April, 1976.

A study of the basic characteristics and needs of
rural and urban elderly residents of Guilford County,
North Carolina. Four hundred sixty nine (469) persons
65 years or older were interviewed in 1970 and 1971.

450. Kivett, Vira R., and C. Bishop. "Characteristics and
needs of persons 65 years and older in Guilford County,
North Carolina." Technical Report #6. Raleigh, North Carolina: University of North Carolina, Home Economics Center
for Research, October, 1973.

451. Kivett, Vira R., and Jean P. Scott. "The Rural By-
passed Elderly: Perspectives on Status and Needs." Technical Bulletin, #260. Greensboro, North Carolina: University of North Carolina, September, 1979.

This monograph reports data on the 418 elderly persons
living in a low income, under served rural North Carolina county. Most of the information is descriptive
and covers topics such as employment, income, housing,
health, subjective well-being, program use, transportation, and recreational activities.

452. Kohles, Mary K., et. al. Project Rural Alive: An
Evaluation Research Project. Lincoln, Nebraska: NCOA,
University of Nebraska, May, 1973.

453. Krout, John A., and David L. Larson. "Self Assessed
Needs of the Rural Elderly." Paper presented at the Annual
Meeting of the Rural Sociological Society (Ithaca, New York:
August, 1980).

Examines the self assessed needs of 5,700 elderly residents living in a northeast nonmetropolitan county.
Analysis of responses to questions on health, access
to medical care and transportation, and adequacy of
income and housing reveals low levels of self identified need. City residents, those under seventy, females, and those living alone generally report the
greatest needs.

454. Kushman, John E., and James Fujii. "Needs Assessment Among Older Rural Americans in the West." Paper presented at a conference on Research and Public Service with the Rural Elderly at the Western Rural Development Center, Oregon State University (Corvallis, Oregon; October, 1980).

> One percent of the elderly in seven counties in California were interviewed in their homes to explore respondents' life satisfaction, problems, and service knowledge and use. Since this is a preliminary report, little in-depth data analysis is presented.

455. Lanham, Karen. See entry number 419.

456. Larson, Donald K., and E. Grant Youmans. "Problems of Rural Elderly Households in Powell County, Kentucky." ERS 665. Washington, D. C.: United States Department of Agriculture, 1978.

> Examines the relationship of household composition and income, transportation, and housing needs with data from questionnaires administered to 252 rural Kentucky households in 1975. Many of the elderly households reported a need for home repair but lacked the assets to make them.

457. Lassey, Marie L., William R. Lassey, and Gary R. Lee. "Elderly People in Rural America." Paper presented at a conference on Research and Public Service with the Rural Elderly at the Western Rural Development Center, Oregon State University (Corvallis, Oregon; October, 1980).

> Outlines the present status, problems, and needs of the rural elderly. Particular attention is paid to: economic status, housing, transportation, employment, health and medical care, social participation, and well-being. Discusses strengths and weaknesses of available services and programs.

458. Laurie, W. See entry number 753.

459. Lipman, Aaron. "Needs Inconsistency of the Rural Aged." Paper presented at a workshop on Rural Gerontology Research in the Northeast at the Northeast Regional Center for Rural Development, Cornell University (Ithaca, New York; May, 1977).

> Argues that needs are of two dimensions: instrumental and expressive. Rural social programs should try to preserve positive expressive features of the rural community.

460. McKain, Walter C., Jr., and H. R. Rosencranz. "Aging in Rural Connecticut." University of Connecticut Research Work Unit/Project Abstract CONS 00356. Storrs, Connecticut: Department of Rural Sociology, University of Connecticut, 1974.

Examines characteristics and problems of the rural
elderly. Suggests possible solutions.

461. Montgomery, James E. See entry number 310.

462. Mulholland, H. B. "Rural Aspects of the Problem of
Aging." National Conference on Rural Health, 12:66-69 (1957).

463. Myllymaki, Judy, and John Wiley. <u>Survey of Needs of
Persons Age 60 and Over in Five Rural Counties of Northeastern Montana</u>. Helena, Montana: Montana Department of Social
and Rehabilitation Services, 1974.

Presents demographic characteristics and perceived and
actual problems of the rural elderly of Montana. Data
are from interviews with 690 residents.

464. National Center on the Black Aged. See entry number 424.

465. National Council on the Aging. "The Rural Elderly."
<u>Perspective on Aging</u>, 9(4):20-24 (July/August, 1980).

A brief discussion of the status of the rural elderly
and recommendations of the National Council on the
Aging to deal with problems facing the rural aged.
Covers income, health, transportation, housing, senior
centers, minorities, and women.

466. New York Senate Research Service. "Old Age and Rural-
ism...A Case of Double Jeopardy. A Report on the Rural Elderly." Albany, New York: New York State Senate, May, 1980.

Reviews the characteristics of the rural elderly and
rural places. Discusses the impact of specific problem areas; transportation, income, and service delivery. Data cited from entire nation but the focus is
on New York State.

467. Powers, R. C. See entry number 316.

468. Richard, Terry Trevino. See entry number 771.

469. Riley, Patricia. "Needs Assessment and the Rural Elderly: A Political Perspective." Paper presented at a workshop on Rural Gerontology Research in the Northeast at the
Northeast Regional Center for Rural Development, Cornell
University (Ithaca, New York; May, 1977).

Sketches Maine's experience in assessing the needs of
its elderly and notes the difficulty of responding ap-
propriately to needs in light of 'political realities'.

470. Rosen, Catherine E. "A comparison of black and white
rural elderly." Athens, Georgia: Northeastern Georgia
Community Mental Health Center, 1977.

471. Saltzman, Ben N. See entry number 198.

472. Sell, Ted. "Problems of Aging: The Elderly Rule Small Towns." Small Town, 5:5-7 (1974).

473. Sotomayor, Martha. " The Rural Elderly." In Paul K. H. Kim and C. P. Wilson (eds.), Toward Mental Health of the Rural Elderly. Washington, D. C.: University Press of America, 1981. Pp. 31-51.

> Using 1970 Census data the author presents information on the needs and lifestyles of the rural elderly. Topics include: demographic characteristics, economic factors, housing, health and nutrition, social isolation, transportation, employment, and recommendations for meeting needs in these areas.

474. Steele, G. Alec. "Interpersonal Involvement as a Coping Resource in a Rural Retirement Community." Paper presented at the 30th Annual Meeting of the Gerontological Society of America (San Francisco, California; November, 1977).

> This paper examines the problems experienced by retirees moving to rural Florida and their disappointment when what they find is not what they had envisioned. Also talks about how they attempt to cope with these feelings.

475. Taietz, Philip. See entry number 778.

476. United States Department of Commerce. National Technical Information Service. Elderly Needs Assessment: Northern Kentucky Area Development District. Washington, D. C.: Economic Development Administration, (June) 1976.

> Describes the procedures used in this elderly needs assessment of a largely rural area and presents its results. The needs data is presented by functional area and on a geographic basis (urban vs. rural and by county). Functional areas covered are: social-psychological, transportation, housing, nutrition, and employment.

477. United States Department of Health, Education, and Welfare, Administration on Aging. Problems of Rural Elderly Household. Washington, D. C.: Administration on Aging, Statistical Note, 3:4-6 (January, 1979).

478. United States House, Committee on Government Operations. Special problems of the rural aging. (House Report #93-103, Vol. 3-5:13022-13025; 93rd Congress, 1st Session.) Washington, D. C.: United States Government Printing Office, April, 1973.

479. United States House, Select Committee on Aging, Sub-

committee on Housing and Consumer Interests. Problems of
the elderly in Nevada. (Hearing, Part I, October 10, Carson
City, Nevada.) Washington, D. C.: United States Government
Printing Office, 1975.

480. United States House, Select Committee on Aging. Problems of the elderly in Fresno, California (rural small
towns). (Hearing, 94th Congress, 1st Session, November 21-
st.) Washington, D. C.: United States Government Printing
Office, 1975.

481. United States House, Select Committee on Aging. Needs
of the rural elderly: a community conference. (95th Congress, August 21st.) Washington, D. C.: United States
Government Printing Office, 1978.

482. United States Senate, Committee on Human Resources,
Subcommittee on Aging. Special needs and problems of older
Americans in rural and small communities. (Hearing, Portland, Maine, 95th Congress, 2nd Session, July 28th.) Washington, D. C.: United States Government Printing Office, 19-
78.

483. United States Senate, Labor and Public Welfare Committee, Subcommittee on Aging. Problems and needs of senior
citizens in rural areas. (94th Congress, 1st Session, December 13th.) Washington, D. C.: United State Government
Printing Office, 1975.

> Testimony of aging spokesman in Vermont.

484. United States Senate, Special Committee on Aging. The
nation's rural elderly part 8, Flagstaff, Arizona. (95th
Congress, 1st Session, November 12th.) Washington, D. C.:
United States Government Printing Office, 1977.

> Using specifics from northern Arizona, this hearing
> examines the following needs and services of the rural
> elderly: transportation, health care, housing, nutri-
> tion, senior center, Older Americans Act, Joint Simpli-
> fication Act and funding.

485. United States Senate, Special Committee on Aging. The
nation's rural elderly part 10, Terre Haute, Indiana. (95th
Congress, 1st Session, November 12th.) Washington, D. C.:
United States Government Printing Office, 1977.

> Focuses on problems unique to the rural elderly. Test-
> imony on Terre Haute, Indiana delves into three main
> areas: services provided under the Older Americans
> Act, energy problems, and health care.

486. United States Senate, Special Committee on Aging. The
nation's rural elderly part 11, Phoenix, Arizona. (95th Congress, 1st Session, November 12th.) Washington, D. C.: United States Government Printing Office, 1977.

Examines problems of the elderly Indian in Arizona including: transportation, housing, income, home care,
and programs that are needed. The Older Americans Act
is discussed in relation to its' funding limitations
to recipients.

487. United States Senate, Special Committee on Aging.
Maine's rural elderly: independence without isolation.
(Hearing, 96th Congress, 2nd Session, June 9th.) Washington,
D. C.: United States Government Printing Office, 1980.

488. Welichs, K. W. See entry number 786.

489. Western Gerontological Society. Generations: A Quarterly Newsletter." Generations, 11(3):entire issue (Fall,
1977).

Half of this issue is devoted to examining problems of
the rural elderly and the policies and services needed
to solve them. Short articles are included on topics
such as transportation, health care, retirement, senior
centers, and in-home service delivery.

490. Wellons, K. W., et. al. "Differential Needs of the
Metropolitan Small Town and Rural Elderly: Service Implications." The Gerontologist, 15(5):96 (1975).

Examines the needs of the elderly living in communities
of differing sizes and discusses the implications of
these needs for service delivery.

NUTRITION

491. Bazzarree, Terry L. "Food Intake Among the Rural Elderly." Paper presented at the 2nd Annual Scientific Meeting
of the Southern Gerontological Association (Atlanta, Georgia;
February, 1981).

Argues that nutrition services to rural elderly are
inadequate. Notes the limited resources and facilities
of rural areas and advocates a multidisciplinary approach to future studies.

492. Bazzarre, Terry L., J. A. Yuhas, R. M. Learner, S. L.
Wu, and V. R. Kivett. "Evaluation of Dietary Survey Metho-
dology Among Rural Elderly." Paper presented at the Annual
Meeting of the Gerontological Society of America (San Diego,
California; November, 1980).

Presents findings from a study of the reliability, validity, and comparability of three methods of assessing
food intake: the 24 hour recall, the diet history,
and the 3-day food record. The data was collected
from 47 rural elderly for six weeks. The advantages
and limitations of each method are discussed.

493. Brown, Martha Susan. "Socio-psychological factors affecting the dietary intake of non-institutionalized rural elderly." (Doctoral dissertation, Florida State University, Tallahassee, Florida, July, 1980.) Dissertation Abstracts International, 40, 1, B, p.135.

> This research examines the relationship between the dietary intake and food preferences of 139 rural North Carolina elderly residents and their education, income, health, mobility, and psychological status.

494. Brown, P. T., J. G. Bergan, E. P. Parson, and I. Krol. "Rural Independent-Living Men and Women vs. Nursing Home Residents." Journal of the American Dietetic Association, 71(1):41-45 (1977).

> Contrasts the diet of rural elderly community residents with that of nursing home residents. Findings are inconclusive because different measuring instruments for each group were used.

495. Glover, Esther E. "Nutrition and the Rural Elderly." In Paul K. H. Kim and C. P. Wilson (eds.), Toward Mental Health of the Rural Elderly. Washington, D. C.: University Press of America, 1981. Pp. 97-116.

> Discusses the nutritional problems of the elderly with emphasis on the rural elderly. Topics include nutritional needs and adequacy and factors affecting the diets of the elderly. Presents the nutritional habits of the rural elderly in southeastern Arkansas. Data are from personal interviews of 80 persons living in small towns.

496. Goldenrod Hills Community Action Council. "Project Rural A. L. I. V. E. (Americans Living in Varied Environments): A Comparative Study of Older Caucasians, Omaha Indians, and Winnebago Indians in No Cost, Nutritions Meals, and Socialization." Grant #93-P-75025. Washington, D. C.: Association on Aging, n. d.

> A feasibility study of nutrition and social interaction programs for the rural elderly living in a Nebraska county.

497. Guthrie, Helen A., Kathleen Black, and J. Patrick Madden. "Nutritional Practices of Elderly Citizens in Rural Pennsylvania." The Gerontologist, 27:330-335 (1972).

> Evaluates the nutritional adequacy of two groups of rural elderly and compares their dietary practices with data from in-home interviews of 99 persons in 70 households.

498. Kim, Paul K. H. See entry number 151.

499. Kinard, J. D. See entry number 388.

500. Learner, R. Max, and Vira R. Kivett. "Discriminators of Perceived Dietary Adequacy Among the Rural Elderly." Journal of the American Dietetic Association, 78:330-337 (April, 1981).

> A secondary analysis of data collected in 1976 from 402 older residents of a rural county in North Carolina. Investigates interrelationships between social, psychological, and health factors affecting perception of dietary adequacy.

501. Madden, J. Patrick (ed.) Research Pertaining to the Elderly: Report of Progress. University Park, Pennsylvania: Department of Agricultural Economics and Rural Sociology, Pennsylvania State University, 1974.

> Examines the utilization of a congregate meals program in Lucerne County, Pennsylvania. Creates an instrument for assessing the independence of elderly people.

502. Oliver, David B. "Nutrition and Health Care." In Robert C. Atchley with Thomas O. Byerts (eds.), Rural Environments and Aging. Washington, D. C.: Gerontological Society, 1975. Pp. 163-184.

> Examines the relationship between health and nutrition. Discusses rural nutritional programs and studies, rural health care, and implications for research and policies.

503. Rawson, Ian G., Edward I. Weinberg, JoAnn Herold, and Judy Holtz. "Nutrition of Rural Elderly in Southwestern Pennsylvania." The Gerontologist, 18:24-29 (1978).

> Reports on a 1975 survey conducted to identify nutritional deficiencies among elderly residents of three counties in southwestern Pennsylvania. Calcium and calorie deficiencies were found. The author discusses changes that could be made in nutrition programs to help correct this problem.

504. Timmereck, Thomas C. "Nutrition Problems: A Survey of the Rural Elderly." Geriatrics, 32:137-140 (October, 1977).

> Presents self-reported nutritional behavior of 3,235 older persons from 21 communities of a rural county in northern Utah and examines factors that affect nutritional status. More than 20 percent of the elderly report they eat alone but only 3 percent do not usually have food from each of the major food groups.

505. Walden, Olivia. "Discussion of David B. Oliver's

Paper 'Nutrition and Health Care'." In Robert C. Atchley
with Thomas O. Byerts (eds.), Rural Environments and Aging.
Washington, D. C.: Gerontological Society, 1975. Pp. 185-
186.

>   Discusses David Oliver's paper noting the strengths
>   of the program he proposes. Argues that because of
>   limited funding, research projects should try to im-
>   prove existing programs rather than create new ones.

506. White, Patricia Smith. "Life quality and mental al-
ertness of rural seniors ranked on nutrient intakes before
supplements." (Doctoral dissertation, University of Maryland, College Park, Maryland, 1981.) Dissertation Abstracts
International, 42, 8, B, p.3185.

>   Examines the relationship between self-reported per-
>   ception of life quality and mental alertness and nu-
>   tritional intake.

507. Wilkinson, Carroll Wetzel. See entry number 178.

508. Wilkinson, Carroll Wetzel. See entry number 179.

POLICIES, PROGRAMS, AND SERVICES

509. Ansello, Edward F. "Special Considerations in Rural
Aging." Educational Gerontology, 5(4):343-354 (October-
December, 1980).

>   The author states the rural elderly have values, needs,
>   and attitudes that differ from the urban elderly and
>   younger rural residents. He argues that these differ-
>   ences have implications for the types of program strat-
>   egies that can be successful in rural areas and that
>   although the rural elderly have lower levels of income,
>   housing, and health care, they tend to have higher
>   levels of life satisfaction.

510. Ambrosius, Richard G. A Report on National Rural Strategy Conference to Improve Service Delivery to the Rural Elderly. Spencer, Iowa: Iowa Lakes Area Agency on Aging, (February) 1979.

>   Proceedings of a conference sponsored by the Farmers
>   Home Administration. Topics include transportation
>   outreach, administration, housing, income, health,
>   and nutrition.

511. Ambrosius, Richard, G. "To Dream the Impossible Dream:
Delivering Coordinated Services to the Rural Elderly." In
Paul K. H. Kim and C. P. Wilson (eds.), Toward Mental Health
of the Rural Elderly. Washington, D. C.: University Press
of America, 1981. Pp. 289-316.

Describes the growth and successes of the Iowa Lakes
Area Agency on Aging which serves 27,000 rural elderly
in nine counties of Northwest Iowa. Extensive discussion of the definition of "rural". Advocates the
coordinated comprehensive service delivery system as
an effective means of providing services to the rural
elderly.

512. Bastida, Elena. See entry number 408.

513. Bazzarre, Terry L. See entry number 491.

514. Beall, George T. See entry number 293.

515. Berry, C. G. See entry number 722.

516. Blake, Brian F., and M. Powell Lawton. "Perceived
Community Functions and the Rural Elderly." *Educational
Gerontology*, 5:375-386 (1980).

Reports data on the ways in which a sample of 336 rural
southern Indiana elderly persons see various community
facilities and services contributing to their well
being (personal maintenance, personal development, and
personal relations and recreation). Illustrates the
usefulness of data on the perceptions of services by
elderly service consumers for program planning.

517. Blonsky, L. E. "An Innovative Service for the Elderly."
The Gerontologist, 13(2):189-196 (1973).

Describes a model for a medical delivery service for
the rural aged.

518. Britton, J. H. "Expectations for Older Persons by
Residents of a Rural Community: Solution of Personal Problems and Uses of Sources of Help." *Journal of Gerontology*,
14:503 (1959).

Nearly 500 adults from a rural Pennsylvania community
were interviewed in 1955 to determine their perceptions
of solutions to older persons' problems and their perceptions on the availability and use of services for
the elderly.

519. Brown, T. E. See entry number 234.

520. Buckholz, Marjorie. "Resident Initiation of Services
in Housing Converted by Rent Subsidy." Paper presented at
the 30th Annual Meeting of the Gerontological Society of
America (San Francisco, California; 1977).

Presents data on rural elderly residents of an apart-
ment complex located in a rural nonfarm county of 60,
000. Describes their use of available services and
activities.

521. Burr, J. J. "Protective Services for Older Adults: A Demonstration Project." Welfare in Review, 9(6):1-6 (1971).

522. Chandler, Suzannah. A Comprehensive Program for the Elderly in Rural Areas. (Revised) Washington, D. C.: National Council on Aging, 1972.

> Describes a model for a rural Community Action Program that incorporates the assistance of the elderly in the fight against poverty. The elderly are involved as staff, service providers, and as planning aides.

523. Correll, S. D. "Difficult services to the elderly." Amherst, New York: Center for the Study of Aging, State University of New York, 1978.

> Presents findings from a study of home health care providers. Problems with rural patients are discussed.

524. Coward, Raymond T. "Planning Community Services for the Rural Elderly: Implications From Research." The Gerontologist, 19:275-282 (1979).

> Argues that the demand for elderly services in rural areas has increased due to demographic changes as well as increased recognition of the needs of the rural elderly. Coward also identifies a number of points that should be kept in mind when planning services for the rural elderly: the diversity found between "rural" environments; the age range of the elderly; the unfound myths about rural persons; and the need to incorporate service delivery programs into existing rural institutions meaningful to the elderly.

525. Coward, Raymond T. "Research-Based Programs for the Rural Elderly." Paper presented at a conference on Research and Public Service with the Rural Elderly at the Western Rural Development Center, Oregon State University (Corvallis, Oregon; October, 1980).

> Stresses the need for rural practitioners to extract from research all available information on the rural elderly. Presents a review and discussion of research on the rural elderly that the author feels is of particular importance for practitioners. Also comments on service delivery to the elderly in rural areas.

526. Coward, Raymond T. "Barriers to Providing Services to the Rural Elderly." Symposium presentation at the Annual Meeting of the Gerontological Society of America (Boston, Massachusetts; November, 1982).

> Focuses on the demographic, organizational, and socio-cultural aspects of rural areas and populations that create barriers to the effective planning and imple-

mentation of formal services to the rural elderly.

527. Coward, Raymond T., and Richard K. Kerckhoff. "The rural elderly: program planning quidelines." Ames, Iowa: North Central Regional Center for Rural Development, Iowa State University, October, 1978.

528. Cozart, E. S. See entry number 358.

529. Cryns, Arthur G., and Abraham Monk. "The Awareness and Need for Social Services: An Area Study." Paper presented at the 28th Annual Meeting of the Gerontological Society of America (Louisville, Kentucky; November, 1975).

Regression analysis is used to identify characteristics of service providers and how these characteristics influence attitudes and behavior toward the elderly. Age is the only significant factor. Younger respondents are found to deal more effectively with older persons.

530. Cryns, Arthur G., and Abraham Monk. "Rural aged: a analysis of key providers of services to the elderly." Buffalo, New York: State University College of New York, 1975.

Final report on a study of New York rural county aging directors.

531. Cryns, Arthur G., and Abraham Monk. "Personal Attributes of Rural Service Providers and Correlates of Role-Effectiveness." Paper presented at the 30th Annual Meeting of the Gerontological Society of America (San Francisco, California; November, 1977).

Examines the relationship between age of service providers and effectiveness in dealing with the elderly. Younger workers are found to have more positive attitudes toward the aged.

532. DeJong, Fred J., and Carol J. Bishop. "Aging: A View From the Country." Paper presented at the 33rd Annual Meeting of the Gerontological Society of America (San Diego, California, November, 1980).

Argues that the rural low income elderly can be characterized by a set of conditions that affect their needs and their access to services designed to meet those needs. These conditions are: higher concentrations of old people, higher average age, greater poverty, and different attitudes towards assistance. Also discusses the rural/urban differences in service providers that are important for rural aged policies.

533. Davenport, Joseph, III. See entry number 242.

534. Decker, James T. See entry number 412.

535. Derr, J. M. "Rural social problems, human services, and social policies." Working Paper 13: Social Services. Denver, Colorado: Center for Social Research and Development, Denver Research Institute, University of Denver, 1973.

     Reports on literature available which exposes obstacles inhibiting the efficient and effective delivery of social services in rural areas. Suggests further social service research and demonstration projects focused on establishing better service delivery systems.

536. Derr, Don A. See entry number 300.

537. Dunkelberger, J. E. "Rural People Aware of Medicare Program." Highlights of Agricultural Research, 15:13 (Winter, 1968).

     Residents of 220 rural farm and non-farm households in five counties of Alabama were surveyed to ascertain their awareness of medicare.

538. Ehrlich, Phyllis Diane. See entry number 342.

539. Enders, W. T., et. al. "Access to essential services in rural/urban environment." Austin, Texas: Council for Advanced Transportation Studies, University of Texas, 1974.

     A bibliography on the accessibility of services to the rural aged such as physical, social, and psychological services.

540. Erwin, William Shafer. "Consumer Participation in Aging Planning: A Case From Rural Arizona." The Gerontologist, 14:245-248 (June, 1974).

     Describes a planning process implemented in rural Arizona. Small groups representative of the elderly citizenry were established to identify needs, solutions, and a plan for meeting the needs of the rural elderly.

541. Farmers Home Administration. "Improving Services for the Rural Elderly." Summary report of the National Strategy Conference on Improving Service to the Rural Elderly, Des Moines, Iowa, United States Department of Agriculture, Washington, D. C. (January 28 - February 2, 1979).

542. Farris, D., G. Rappole, F. Shelton, and J. Bruni. "Introducing Federal Funding for Aging Programs in Rural Counties of North Central Texas: Challenge and Response." The Gerontologist, 17:60 (1977).

     Discusses the implementation of Title VII programs in nine rural Texas counties. Special attention is given to detailing the counties demographic characteristics and their resistance to federal programs.

543. Fauri, David P. "Providing Human Resources for the Rural Elderly." Human Services in the Rural Environment, November-December, 1980.

A discussion of problems facing the rural elderly in areas such as: energy costs, service delivery, and competition for funds. The author's discussion is highlighted by a concern that the rural elderly are lacking an appropriate voice in policy issues.

544. Fleicher, D., et. al. "Outsiders and change: altering services to the elderly in rural communities." Laramie, Wyoming: University of Wyoming, 1974.

545. Frekany, G. A. See entry number 359.

546. Ginsberg, Leon, H., (ed.). Social Work in Rural Communities, A Book of Readings. New York: Council on Social Work Education, 1976.

A collection of articles on social work in rural communities designed as a resource tool for educators and social work practitioners. In depth and detailed, a thorough overview of social work education, educational assumptions, planning for use of available resources, rural mental health, community organizations, rural elderly vs. urban elderly, welfare, news media, and an annotated bibliography on rural social work.

547. Gordon, Jacob U. "Use of Aging Services by Elderly Blacks in Douglas County Kansas." Journal of Minority Aging, 4:88-92 (1979).

A study of service awareness and use among 54 rural Kansas black men. Low levels of service knowledge and use were uncovered with respondents expressing high levels of self support and independence.

548. Grams, Armin. "Legislation and Regulations That Discriminate Against Rural Elders." Paper persented at the Annual Meeting of the National Conference on Aging (Washington, D. C.; April, 1981).

Examines the inequities between urban and rural programs and services for the aged and discusses the effects of local and national legislation and regulations.

549. Gunter, Patricia Lee. See entry number 445.

550. Gullie, R. See entry number 360.

551. Harbert, Anita, and Leon Ginsberg. Human Services for Older Adults: Concepts and Skills. Belmont, California: Wadsworth Publishing Company, 1978.

This book has part of a chapter that deals with the rural elderly.

552. Hayslip, Bert, Jr., Mary Lou Ritter, Ruth M. Oltman, and Connie McDonnell. "Home Care Services and the Rural Elderly." The Gerontologist, 20(2):192-199 (1980).

Perceived home care needs of the rural elderly are compared to agencies' perceptions of needs. Data was collected in 1977 and 1978 from 299 rural older persons and from six area agencies. Elderly respondents indicated substantial needs for home health care services. Data from the agencies showed that income, service accessibility and visibility, inter-agency coordination, and staff priorities were determinants of service quantity and quality.

553. Hess, Clinton. "Insider Input: The Case for Senior Control in Rural Areas." Paper presented at a Workshop on Rural Gerontology Research, Pennsylvania State University (State College, Pennsylvania; May, 1977).

554. Hess, Clinton. "Alternative Organizational Structures." Paper presented at a workshop on Rural Gerontology Research in the Northeast at the Northeast Regional Center for Rural Development, Cornell University (Ithaca, New York; May, 1977).

Argues that if older persons had more input in planning programs, services would be more responsive to needs.

555. Hoffman, Donald H. See entry number 106.

556. Hoppa, Mary E., and Gary D. Roberts. "Implications of the Activity Factor." The Gerontologist, 14(4):331-335 (August, 1974).

This study compares senior center attenders (n=101) and non-attenders in a nonmetropolitan Washington state county on self-reported needs and level of activity.

557. House, Gail, et. al. "Model rural project for home-maker service aide program to the elderly: summary statement and final report." (Prepared by College of Home Economics, Texas Tech University.) Washington, D. C.: The Administration on Aging, United States Department of Health, Education, and Welfare, August, 1978.

558. Hunter, Jon B., Mary W. Macht, and Kevin J. Mahoney. "Amendments of the Older American's Act: Focusing Attention

on the Rural Elderly." Paper presented at the Annaul Meeting of the Gerontological Society of America (San Diego,
California; November, 1980).

> Analyzes the impact of the 1978 amendments of the Old-
> er American's Act to increase the amount of funds
> spent for services to the rural elderly. As a result
> of these amendments, state agencies must spend 105%
> of the 1978 amount for social and nutrition programs
> and multi-purpose senior centers in rural areas.

559. Hutchinson, William J., and John J. Stretch. "Planning for the Rural Elderly: A Case Study of the Seven South-
ernmost Counties in Illinois." Paper presented at the Annual Meeting of the Gerontological Society of America (Toronto, Canada; November, 1981).

> Presents findings from 67 key informants on three areas
> of service to the rural elderly: preventive support
> services, services to meet an acute or crisis episode,
> and services to help an older person adapt, adjust or
> stabilize to a chronic condition or after an acute
> episode. Focuses on the awareness, availability,
> accessibility, and acceptability of these services.

560. Iowa Dial-A-Listener. "County starts 'Telecare' Program." Aging, 199:12 (1971).

> Describes a volunteer service that makes daily check-
> up telephone calls to elderly persons living alone.
> The 'Telecare' service is considered valuable because
> of its direct and nearly exclusive serving of the
> aged.

561. Jacks, M. H. "Social Services for Older People in
Nonurban Areas." In C. C. Osterbird (ed.), Migration, Mo-
bility, and Aging. Gainsville, Florida: The University
Presses of Florida, 1974.

> Identifies and explores four aspects of planning ser-
> vices for the rural elderly: providing services in
> the home, potential sources of service provision and
> methods of service delivery, impact of rural residency
> on need and availability of services, and the effect
> of population mobility on older rural residents and
> their needs.

562. Jirovec, R. "Self-Help Programs Among the Rural Aged."
Paper presented at the Annual Meeting of the Gerontological
Society of America (San Diego, California; November, 1980).

> Describes and evaluates two self-help programs design-
> ed to improve the quality of life of the rural aged.
> Examines the reasons for their success and/or failure.
> The main reason for success was the ability of one

program to integrate into the institutional network of the community.

563. Johnson, David Pittman. See entry number 253.

564. Jones, James R., and Joan D. Jones. "Serving Older Adults in Rural Areas: Approaches to Planning and Implementation." Paper prepared for the Administration on Aging (September 19, 1975).

565. Kaplan, Jerome, and Philip Taietz. "The Rural Aged." Geriatrics, 13:752-757 (November, 1958).

Selected characteristics of rural life are examined in regard to community planning for older people. Authors note that problems of rural aged are very similar to those of their urban counterparts. The differences are in resources for coping with problems. Rural elderly tend to have stronger family support, but lack the formal networks available to city dwellers.

566. Karcher, Charles J., and Barbara C. Karcher. "Higher Education and Religion: Potential Partners in Service to the Rural Elderly." Educational Gerontology, 5(4):409-421 (1980).

Argues that the church is already a trusted institution for the rural elderly and could be used to help provide continuing education services, develop community services and facilities, and conduct research on the elderly's needs.

567. Kerckhoff, Richard K., and Raymond T. Coward. "Delivering Human Services to the Rural Edlerly: Implications From Research." Paper presented at the Annual Conference of the National Council on Family Relations (San Diego, California; October, 1977).

Identifies five dimensions reflecting implications of available research for practitioners: diversity in rural communities, aging as a period of growth, myths about the rural elderly, cooperation in rural communities, and family-oriented programming.

568. Kim, Paul K. H. See entry number 151.

569. Kim, Paul K. H. "The Low Income Rural Elderly: Under Served Victims of Public Inequity." Paper presented at Community Service Administration Symposium, University of Kentucky (Lexington, Kentucky; 1980).

A discussion of the ways in which public policy discriminates against the rural elderly in areas of need such as income, health and mental health, housing, and transportation. Cites specific program and program

outlays and makes recommendations as to how such inequities could be addressed.

570. Kim, Paul K. H. "Predicaments in Aging Services as
Perceived by MSW Social Workers in Rural Areas." Paper presented at the Annual Meeting of the Gerontological Society
of America (Toronto, Canada; November, 1981).

Reports findings from a survey of some 300 recent MSW's
that identifies the characteristics of rural settings
that have negative consequences for the delivery of
service to rural elderly clients. Author argues that
MSW's working in rural areas want to improve their
knowledge and skills but little training opportunities
exist in rural-oriented service delivery systems.

571. Kim, Paul K. H., and John R. Ballantine. "Awakening
of the Rural Aging: An Interdisciplinary Social Work -
Rural Aging Training and Program Development Project." In
Joseph Davenport III, et. al. (eds.), Social Work in Rural
Areas: Issues and Opportunities. Laramie, Wyoming: Uni-
versity of Wyoming, 1979.

572. Kimbee, Phillip. "Rural Aging Policy. Who Needs It?"
Generations (Western Gerontological Society), Fall:8 (1977).

Kimbee argues that a national rural aging policy is
needed to ensure that the rural elderly get their fair
share of money and services. Such a policy should give
special consideration to rural conditions and be developed from the local level up.

573. Kraig, Bonnie. "Technology of New Rural Society; A
Legacy of Peter C. Goldmark." Perspective on Aging, 7(1):
16-18 (1978).

A short article describing creative ways to meet the
needs of the isolated rural elderly such as mobile
vans with remote hook-up to a hospital and adult education programs on tape.

574. Kretz, S. E. See entry number 255.

575. Krout, John A., and David Larson. "Service utilization
patterns of the rural elderly." Final report to the Administration on Aging (December, 1980).

Analyzes data on service utilization patterns of some
5,700 elderly residing in a northeast nonmetropolitan
county. Also examines the impact of a needs assessment survey on the elderly's use of services.

576. Krout, John A. "Service Utilization Patterns of the
Rural Elderly." Paper presented at the Annaul Meeting of
the Rural Sociological Society (Guelph, Canada; August, 1981).

This paper examined service utilization among a sample
of 5,700 over sixty residents of a New York nonmetropolitan county. Twenty percent of the sample reported
using at least one of the six services covered by the
survey. Service utilization rates were found to be
significantly higher for those elderly over seventy,
not married, living alone, and having lower levels of
education and income. No differences for service usage
between residents of the open country, villages, or
urban places emerged.

577. Krout, John A. "Service Utilization by the Elderly: A
Critical Review of the Literature." Paper presented at the
Annual Meeting of the Gerontological Society of America (Tor-
onto, Canada; November, 1981).

A general review of the knowledge and use of social
services by the elderly with a section devoted specifically to the rural elderly. Criticizes the substantive
and methodological short comings of this literature and
suggests ways to improve work in this area.

578. Krout, John A. "The Structure of Service Delivery in
Rural vs. Urban Areas: Implications for Informal Networks."
Paper presented at the Annual Meeting of the National Confer-
ence on Aging (Washington, D. C.; April, 1982).

Argues that the lack of adequate formal service delivery systems for the rural elderly increases the need
for the development and support of a strong system of
informal networks.

579. Krout, John A. "Determinants of service use by the
aged." Final report to the NRTA-AARP Andrus Foundation
(June, 1982).

An analysis of in depth personal interviews with 250
elderly living in a small city. Examines degree and
sources of knowledge and correlates of use of community services with special attention to a local senior
center. Knowledge and use of the center and services
was found to be quite low although center participants
were more knowledgeable of programs.

580. Krout, John A. "The Rural Elderly: Issues in Service
Provision and Utilization." Paper presented at the Annual
Meeting of the Rural Sociological Society (San Francisco,
California; September, 1982).

Discusses the demography and needs of the rural elderly
and their implications for service provision. Also
presents a critical look at the inadequacies and draw-
backs of existing formal services as they exist in
rural areas.

581. Krout, John A. "Rural Elderly: Service Availability,

Accessibility, and Utilization." Paper presented at the Annual Meeting of the New York State Association of Gerontological Educators (Grossinger's, New York; October, 1982).

> Reviews the existing literature on the availability,
> accessibility, and use of services for the rural elder-
> ly.

582. Krout, John A. "Correlates of Senior Center Participation." Paper presented at the Annual Meeting of the Gerontological Society of America (Boston, Massachusetts; November, 1982).

> Reports on the correlates of senior center utilization
> for a sample of 250 small city residents living in a
> New York nonmetropolitan county. Center users were
> found to have lower levels of education, income, self-
> assessed health, and mobility.

583. Kushman, John E. See entry number 454.

584. LeRay, Nelson L., Don A. Derr, and E. F. Jensen, Jr.
"Elderly Households in the Nonmetropolitan Northeast and
Their Satisfaction with Community Services." Research Bul-
letin Number 646; March, 1977. Amherst, Massachusetts: Mas-
sachusetts Agricultural Experimental Station, University of
Massachusetts, USDA Economic Research Service, 1977.

> Describes several socio-economic characteristics of
> 662 households in the northeast and reports on satis-
> faction with community services.

585. LeRay, Nelson L., Charles O. Crawford, Dennis A. Wat-
kins, and Don A. Derr. "Community Services for Older People
in the Rural Northeast." Paper presented at a workshop on
Rural Gerontology Research in the Northeast at the Northeast
Regional Center for Rural Development, Cornell University
(Ithaca, New York; May, 1977).

> Determines the extent of research on the rural elderly
> and the amount of data available from agencies serving
> the rural elderly. Examines agencies' interest in
> research. Refines data collection and analysis tech-
> niques and develops informational networks.

586. Lassey, Marie L. See entry number 457.

587. Learner, R. Max. See entry number 257.

588. Leondedis, G. P. "A Special Kind of Villa." H.U.D.
Challenge, May, 1975.

> This short article provides an overview of a multi-
> purpose center serving the needs of the rural elderly.

589. Linstrom, R. C. "A Linkage Point for Health and Social

Services." The Gerontologist, 10(2):107-110 (1970).

> This paper discusses alternative modes of coordinating
> services for the rural elderly.

590. Lipman, Aaron. See entry number 459.

591. Lohmann, Nancy. "Research on the Rural Aged: Implications for Social Work Practice." Third National Conference on Rural Social Work, August, 1978.

> A review of the literature in four areas dealing with
> the rural elderly: demography, family, social rela-
> tionships, and quality of life. Discusses the im-
> plications of research findings on these topics for
> social work practitioners.

592. Lohmann, Nancy, and Roger Lohmann. "Urban-Designed
Programs for the Rural Aged: Are They Exportable?" In R. K.
Green and S. A. Webster (eds.), Effective Models for the
Delivery of Services in Rural Areas: Implications for Prac-
tice and Social Work Education. Knoxville, Tennessee: Uni-
versity of Tennessee School of Social Work, 1976 (July).

593. Lohmann, Nancy, Roger Lohmann, and Ellen F. Netting.
"Social Work Practice With the Rural Aged." In Paul K. H.
Kim and C. P. Wilson (eds.), Toward Mental Health of the Rural Elderly. Washington, D. C.: University Press of America, 1981. Pp. 283-288.

> Presents three factors important to the delivery of
> services to the rural elderly: their needs, the type
> of programs required, the delivery of services. In-
> cludes implications for social work practice.

594. Lohmann, Roger A. "The Politics of Aging and Rural
Social Services." Paper presented at the 3rd Annual Institute on Rural Social Work (Morgantown, West Virginia; August,
1978).

595. Lohmann, Roger A. "Planning for Aging Services: Im-
plications of Recent Amendments to the Older Americans Act."
Paper presented at the Annual Meeting of the Gerontological
Society of America (Toronto, Canada; November, 1981).

> Identifies important provisions of amendments to the
> Older Americans Act. Argues that the common interpre-
> tation of these provisions ignores many key questions
> for planning. Examines service systems for the aged
> in communities in seven counties of West Virginia.

596. Lohmann, Roger A. "Comprehensive What? Coordination
of Whom? Rural AAA's and the Planning Mandate." Paper
presented at the Annual Meeting of the Gerontological Society of America (Toronto, Canada; November, 1981).

Considers the system of rural planning which has developed in the United States. The original plan of congress of a regional planning network has failed to materialize. Suggests ways to make regional planning work.

597. McConatha, Douglas, J. Howsden, and B. Pinckard. "The service utilization myth: the case of the rural black elderly." Jacksonville, Alabama: State University of Alabama, 1979.

598. McCoy, John F., Bernal Green, and Mary Jo Grinstead. "Sixty-Nine Percent of Arkansans Indicate Willingness to Use Services of Physician Extenders." AHSC Technological Reports, 4:1-4 (1974).

Examines characteristics of those willing to use physician extenders to provide health care. The elderly are less willing to use their services.

599. Madden, J. Patrick. See entry number 501.

600. Maki, W. R. See entry number 260.

601. Match, S. K. Participation of Elderly Poor in Senior Centers. Washington, D. C.: National Council on Aging, (SOS Monograph #3) 1970.

602. Maurer, Richard C. See entry number 763.

603. Maurer, Richard, C., James A. Christenson, and Paul D. Warner. "Community Services and the Elderly." In Paul K. H. Kim and C. P. Wilson (eds.), Toward Mental Health of the Rural Elderly. Washington, D. C.: University Press of America, 1981. Pp. 127-142.

Compares the elderly's perceptions of community services to that of younger adults and public officials. Also compares the perceptions among various groups of the elderly. Explores the needs of the elderly in the following areas: health, law enforcement, transportation, recreation, housing, public assistance, and citizen participation. Data are from statewide surveys of residents and public officials.

604. Means, Gary, Joseph Mann, and David Van Dyk. "Reaching Out to the Rural Elderly-Services to Rural America." Human Services in the Rural Environment, 3:1-5 (February, 1978).

Examines barriers to service utilization as 122 elderly persons from rural Arizona perceive them. Data were collected in 1975. Three major barriers were identified: transportation, poor health, and self-identity.

605. Mickey, Callie Parker. "Helping skills in the implementation of the project to assist the rural aged: effectiveness of a micro-training model." (Doctoral dissertation,
Texas Tech University, Lubbock, Texas, February, 1982.)
Dissertation Abstracts International, 42, 8, A, p.3387.

> This study examined the effect of micro-training on
> the basic attending skills of volunteers and profes-
> sionals serving the rural elderly. Experimental and
> control groups were used. The experimental group
> scored higher on helping skills than the control but
> did not show more positive attitudes toward aging or
> the needs of the elderly.

606. Mitchell, M. M. "Service Delivery to the Rural Elderly." Paper presented at the 32nd Annual Meeting of the Gerontological Society of America (Washington, D. C.; November,
1979).

607. Moe, Edward O. "Agency Collaboration in Planning and
Service: The Emerging Network on Aging." Paper presented
at a Workshop on Rural Gerontology Research, Pennsylvania
State University (State College, Pennsylvania; May, 1977).

> Looks back at what has been done to develop service
> networks, examines their present status, and looks
> forward to what can be done to achieve agency colla-
> boration.

608. Moen, Elizabeth. "The Reluctance of the Elderly to
Accept Help." Social Problems, 25(3):293-303 (February, 19-
78).

> This paper explores the questions of how the needs of
> the rural elderly can be assessed and why the rural
> elderly do not make use of available programs and
> services. Analyzing data from in-depth interviews
> with 25 rural Oregon residents, the author argues that
> a "non-acceptor syndrome" characterizes the rural el-
> derly, particularly the older elderly. This syndrome
> involves a striving toward independence, hostility to-
> ward welfare, refusal to use needed services, and even
> a denial of acceptance of assistance actually given.

609. Monk, A., and A. G. Cryns. "Service Needs of the Rural Elderly: A Comparative Study of Agency Personnel and
Public Officials." Paper presented at the Annual Meeting of
the Gerontological Society of America (New York, New York;
October, 1976).

610. Mountain States Health Corporation. See entry number 263.

611. National Council on the Aging. "Bringing Services to

People in Rural Areas. Senior Centers: Realizing Our Potential." Proceedings of the 8th National Conference of Senior Centers, 1975.

612. National Council on the Aging. NCOA Public Policy Agenda 1979-1980. Washington, D. C.: NCOA, March, 1979.

Intended to encourage responsiveness to the needs and capabilities of older Americans. One section devoted specifically to rural elderly.

613. National Institute of Senior Centers. Senior Center Report 2:6 (July-August). Washington, D. C.: National Council on the Aging, Inc., 1979.

This issue of the Senior Center Report is devoted largely to the rural elderly. Includes short articles on rural senior centers, public transportation for rural areas, and The National Council on the Aging's Center on Rural Aging.

614. Neely, Margery A., et. al. "Cooperative Services for the Rural Frail Elderly." Paper presented at the American Personnel and Guidance Association (1981).

Describes a door-to-door information program designed to advise the rural elderly about services available to them.

615. Nelson, Gary. See entry number 767.

616. Nelson, Gary. See entry number 768.

617. New York State Office for the Aging. Indentification of Barriers Report. Phase 1 of the Rural Aging Services Project. Albany, New York: New York State Office for the Aging, 1982.

This report was developed as part of an AoA funded three year project conducted in New York State to improve services for the rural elderly. It presents the findings from a survey of local service providers operating in rural areas. Transportation, housing, and health and human services are covered. The following major barriers to service provision to the rural elderly were identified: the urban bias of laws and regulations, lack of expertise of rural providers, excessive paper work and report requirements, unresponsive local governments, lack of funds for programs, and negative attitudes of the rural elderly toward soical service programs.

618. New York Senate Research Service. See entry number 466.

619. Noll, P. F. See entry number 314.

620. Norris, Jean. "Multipurpose Centers in a Rural County." Aging and Work: A Journal on Age, Work, and Retirement, 18-20 (May/June, 1978).

     Describes programs and services (medical, educational,
     recreation, nutrition, and transportation) offered
     by multipurpose senior centers in Franklin County,
     New York, a rural county with a population of 40,000.

621. Older American Reports. See entry number 770.

622. Oriol, William E. "The Federal Perspective: New Directions in Rural Gerontology." Paper presented at a workshop on Rural Gerontology Research in the Northeast at the
Northeast Regional Center for Rural Development, Cornell
University (Ithaca, New York; May, 1977).

     Discusses a number of areas important to the well
     being of the rural elderly that receive significant
     federal support and comments on recent legislative
     developments in these areas. Areas covered include
     social security, medicare and medicaid, and housing.

623. Ossofsky, Jack, Executive Director of the National
Council on Aging. "Aging in Rural Mid-America: Are We Up
to the Challenge?" In Lloyd Foerster (ed.), The Aging in
Rural Mid-America: A Symposium on Values for an Evolving
Quality of Life. Lindsberg, Kansas: Bethany College, 19-
78. Pp. 37-47.

     Presents a review of some major trends in aging and
     rural areas in America and discusses some of the
     popular "myths" of aging.

624. Overland, Shirley. "South Dakota Senior Center: A
Growing Experience." Generations (Western Gerontological
Society), Fall:23-24 (1977).

     This brief article discusses the programs of a multi-
     purpose senior center located in rural South Dakota.
     Special attention is paid to a lifelong educational
     program.

625. Parenti, F. R. See entry number 315.

626. Paringer, Lynn. See entry number 215.

627. Parkinson, Larry. "Improving the Delivery of Health
Services to the Rural Elderly: A Policy Perspective." In
Paul K. H. Kim and C. P. Wilson (eds.), Toward Mental Health
of the Rural Elderly." Washington, D. C.: University Press
of America, 1981. Pp. 223-238.

     Argues that the disparity in adequacy of service pro-
     vision to rural and urban areas has been created by

programs and policies that fail to take into account
the unique problems of the rural elderly. Presents
problems of rural elderly in obtaining health care
and suggests solutions.

628. Pickard, Larry. See entry number 269.

629. Powers, Edward A. See entry number 10.

630. Rathbone-McCuan, Eloise. "A Step Toward Integrated
Health and Mental Health Planning for the Rural Elderly." In
Paul K. H. Kim and C. P. Wilson (eds.), Toward Mental Health
of the Rural Elderly. Washington, D. C.: University Press
of America, 1981. Pp. 257-273.

> Contends that the paucity of empirical data documenting
> the needs of the rural elderly adversely affects plan-
> ning efforts. Examines in some depth the health plan-
> ning processes of Missouri. Makes recommendations for
> improving those processes.

631. Reid, Richard A. See entry number 270.

632. Riley, Patricia. See entry number 469.

633. Rosen, Catherine E., and S. Rosen. "An Evaluation of
Improved Services for Senior Center Participants in Rural
Georgia." Report on Grant 90-A-1159(01). Washington, D. C.:
Administration on Aging, Office of Human Development Services,
Department of Health, Education, and Welfare, 1979.

634. Rosen, Catherine E. See entry number 272.

635. Rosen, Catherine E., Robert J. Vanderberg, and Sidney
Rosen. "The Fate of Senior Center Dropouts." In Paul K. H.
Kim and C. P. Wilson (eds.), Toward Mental Health of the
Rural Elderly. Washington, D. C.: University Press of Am-
erica, 1981. Pp. 143-163.

> A longitudinal study investigating reasons for drop-
> ping out of senior centers, the impact of dropping out
> on current functioning, and the influence of rural and
> urban residence upon the drop-outs' well-being. Data
> are from interviews of poverty level rural and urban
> elderly before they joined a senior center and again
> three years later after they had stopped attending the
> center.

636. Rural America Staff. "The Rural Elderly." Paper
presented at the strategies for Rural Action Conference, the
3rd National Conference on Rural America (December, 1977).

637. Schneider, Mary Jo, Diana M. Danforth, and Donald E.
Voth. "Senior Center Participation: A Two-Stage Approach to
Impact Evaluation." Paper presented at the Annaul Meeting

of the Rural Sociological Society (Ithaca, New York; August, 1980).

    Examines determinants of senior center participation and impact on institutionalization, health, life out-look, and use of other available services in two rural Arkansas counties. Four hundred fifty six (456) persons from two rural, low-income counties in Arkansas were interviewed before and after the establishment of social programs for the elderly. The study found that partici-pants were generally not likely to need institutional-ization. Participants also did not differ from non-participants in institutionalization, health, life outlook, or use of other services.

638. Scott, Warren. "The Cooperative Extension Service: Its Role in Reaching and Meeting the Needs of Rural Older Americans." In Paul K. H. Kim and C. P. Wilson (eds.), To-ward Mental Health of the Rural Elderly. Washington, D. C.: University Press of America, 1981. Pp. 337-350.

    Describes the history and objectives of the Cooperative Extension Service in Missouri and other parts of the United States. Emphasizes University of Missouri pro-grams on the aging.

639. Sebastian, Margaret. "In-Service Training For Work With Elderly in Rural Areas." Human Services in the Rural Environment, 3:25-30 (May, 1976).

    Argues that urban methods and strategies are not neces-sarily effective in rural areas. Describes the in-service training program of the University of Minneso-ta - Duluth. Includes a list of examples of training needs for rural practitioners.

640. Shanas, Ethel. See entry number 275.

641. Sheps, Cecil G., and Miriam Bachar. "Rural Areas and Personal Health Services: Current Strategies." American Journal of Public Health, 71:71-82 (Supplement) (January, 1981).

    Delves into the complex issues involved in providing good quality and socially acceptable rural health services. Notes that rural areas suffer from a lack of doctors and an under-utilization of medical services. Also reviews rural health care programs and different strategies of health care provision. Concludes with a list of major policy concerns for which research is needed.

642. Sias, John D. See entry number 277.

643. Smitson, Walter S. See entry number 278.

644. Southern Regional Education Board Manpower Education
and Training Project Rural Task Force. "Educational Assumptions for Rural Social Work." In L. H. Ginsberg (ed.), Social Work in Rural Communities. New York, New York: Council
on Social Work Education, 1976. Pp. 41-44.

> A list of statements outlining characteristics of rural
> America, common problems encountered by practitioners
> in rural areas, formal and informal rural programs,
> gaps in services, and desirable characteristics of
> rural social workers.

645. Steinberg, Raymond M. "Functional Components and Organ-
izational Issues in Rural Service Systems for the Aged: A
Framework for Discussion." Paper presented at a workshop on
Rural Gerontology Research in the Northeast at the Northeast
Regional Center for Rural Development, Cornell University
(Ithaca, New York; May, 1977).

> Asserts that researchers often seem out of touch with
> reality in the field of aging but could make an impor-
> tant contribution by identifying successful models of
> service and by clarifying the conditions under which
> various models do or do not work.

646. Steinhauer, Marcia B. "Obstacles to the Mobilization
and Provision of Services to the Rural Elderly." Educational
Gerontology, 5(4):399-408 (October, 1980).

> Three types of obstacles to provision of services are
> described: administrative, logistical, and compliance.
> The author suggests that existing rural values and
> institutions can be utilized to surmount these obsta-
> cles. Examples are employing retired elderly in pro-
> grams, working through non-aging organizations such as
> the Cooperative Extension Service, and tapping infor-
> mal support networks to participate in service deli-
> very.

647. Stojanovic, Elizabeth J. "The Dissemination of Information About Medicare to Low-Income Rural Residents." Rural
Sociology, 37:253-260 (June, 1972).

> Ascertains the channels of communication most likely
> to have provided information about Medicare to low-
> income rural residents. Interviews were administered
> to 769 homemakers from low-income areas in four south-
> eastern states: Alabama, Mississippi, North Carolina,
> and Tennessee. The large majority of respondents had
> heard of the program but blacks were four times as
> likely to be unaware of it than whites. While radio
> and television were the most widespread sources of
> information, a wide variety of media were utilized.

648. Taietz, Philip. "Community Facilities and Social Ser-

vices." In Robert C. Atchley with Thomas O. Byerts (eds.), Rural Environments and Aging. Washington, D. C.: Gerontological Society, 1975. Pp. 145-156.

> Discusses the relationship between community structure and the kinds of service institutions places of various size and organizational complexity possess. Rural places are found to have facilities and services that are less available and accessibility, of lower quality, and more expensive than urban communities.

649. Taietz, Philip. See entry number 780.

650. Tancredi, Lawrence R. See entry number 281.

651. Taves, Marvin J. "Comments on Community Facilities and Social Services." In Robert C. Atchley with Thomas O. Byerts (eds.), Rural Environments and Aging. Washington, D. C.: Gerontological Society, 1975. Pp. 157-161.

> Critiques and expands upon the ideas presented by Philip Taietz in his paper "Community Facilities and Social Services."

652. Taves, Marvin J., and Gary D. Hansen. "Programs for the Rural Elderly." In E. Grant Youmans (ed.), Older Rural Americans. Lexington, Kentucky: University of Kentucky Press, 1967. Pp. 281-303.

> Discusses early and more recent attempts to help the rural elderly such as: social security, medical assistance, and old-age assistance. Also provides examples of community programs for the rural aged and notes special features of rural life that make participation difficult for some rural elderly.

653. Tsutras, Frank G. "Congressional Rural Caucus." Perspective on Aging, 7(1):5,37 (January/February, 1978).

654. United States Department of Agriculture and Farmers Home Administration. Improving services for the rural elderly. Washington, D. C., October, 1980.

655. United States Department of Health, Education, and Welfare Administration. Office on Aging. A rural county cares for its aging, patterns for progress in aging, Case Study #17. Washington, D. C.: Welfare Administration Office of Aging, 1964.

656. United States House, Select Committee on Aging. Services for the elderly in Muskogee, Oklahoma. (Nutritional, senior centers, housing and transportation for a rural area of Oklahoma.) (94th Congress, 2nd Session, May 15th.) Washington, D. C.: United States Government Printing Office, 1976.

657. United States House, Select Committee on Aging, Sub-committee on Federal, State, and Community Services. Older Americans Act programs: a rural perspective. (95th Congress, 1st Session, Huron, North Dakota, December 9th.) Washington, D. C.: United State Government Printing Office, 1977.

658. United States House. See entry number 283.

659. United States House, Select Committee on Aging. Federal programs for the elderly in Kentucky: success or failure? (Hearing, July 6th.) Washington, D. C.: United States Government Printing Office, 1979.

660. United States House. See entry number 284.

661. United States Senate. See entry number 483.

662. United States Senate, Special Committee on Aging. The Older Americans Act and the rural elderly. (Hearing, 94th Congress, 1st Session, April.) Washington, D. C.: United State Government Printing Office, 1975.

663. United States Senate. See entry number 484.

664. United States Senate, Special Committee on Aging. The nation's rural elderly part 9, Tucson, Arizona. (95th Congress, 1st Session, November 12th.) Washington, D. C.: United States Government Printing Office, 1977.

    Examines some of the many services available to the rural elderly of southern Arizona, specifically: transportation, health services, housing, nutrition programs, senior centers , Older Americans Act, funding and volunteer efforts.

665. United States Senate, Special Committee on Aging. Rural elderly - the isolated population: a look at services in the 80's. (Hearing, 96th Congress, 2nd Session, April 11th.) Washington, D. C.: United States Government Printing Office, 1980.

666. Washington, Becky. See entry number 286.

667. Weller, Margaret Ann. See entry number 369.

668. Wellons, K. W. See entry number 490.

669. Wiles, Marilyn M. "Providing Human Services to the Rural Elderly: A State Level Perspective." In Paul K. H. Kim and C. P. Wilson (eds.), Toward Mental Health of the Rural Elderly. Washington, D. C.: University Press of America, 1981. Pp. 239-255

    Focusing on the programs of the Administration on Aging this chapter examines service delivery for the elderly in the United States. Explores the responsibilities of the states in providing services to the rural elderly.

670. Wilkinson, Carroll Wetzel. See entry number 178.

671. Wilkinson, Carroll Wetzel. See entry number 179.

672. Williams, William E., and Sam Garro. "The Green Thumb Program: Building Rural America Through Employment and Services (A History of the New Jersey Unit)." In Paul K. H. Kim and C. P. Wilson (eds.), Toward Mental Health of the Rural Elderly. Washington, D. C.: University Press of America, 1981. Pp. 329-336.

Describes the Green Thumb Program focusing on rural New Jersey. Outlines needs of the rural elderly and shows how the Green Thumb Program has met some of those needs. Suggests areas for expansion of the program.

673. Wilson, Albert J. E., III. "Implementation and Evaluation." Paper presented at a workshop on Rural Gerontology Research in the Northeast at the Northeast Regional Center for Rural Development, Cornell University (Ithaca, New York; May, 1977).

Explores alternative strategies and approaches to meeting the needs of the elderly.

674. Wilson, Constance P. "Training Personnel for Work With the Rural Elderly." In Paul K. H. Kim and C. P. Wilson (eds.), Toward Mental Health of the Rural Elderly. Washington, D. C.: University Press of America, 1981. Pp. 405-409.

Describes a three - year demonstration and training project done at the University of Kentucky from 1978 to 1981. Emphasis of the project was on sensitizing mental health professionals to work with the rural elderly. Includes a list of the needs of the service trainees.

675. Windley, Paul G., and R. J. Scheidt. "Community Services in Small Rural Towns: Patterns of Use By Older Residents." Paper presented at the 35th Annual Meeting of the Gerontological Society of America (Boston, Massachusetts, November, 1982).

Examines utilization of 15 community services by the elderly in 18 small Kansas towns through interviews with 989 elderly individuals. Distance to services was found to be negatively correlated with frequency of service use but the authors argue the data do not support the idea of the rural elderly being isolated.

676. Yang, Yue-Eng. See entry number 356.

677. Ybarra, G. See entry number 792.

RESEARCH METHODS

678.   Bazzarree, T. L.   See entry number 492.

679.   Gardner, Margaret Ann.   "Caring and Sharing."   Perspective on Aging, X(1):4-7 (January/February, 1981).

This paper discusses the applicability of anthropological field methods to the study of the rural elderly. The author identifies ways in which the rural elderly view their surroundings and their place in the community.

680.   Hanreider, B. D.   See entry number 38.

681.   Lamprey, Headlee.   "Research on the Rural Elderly." In Paul K. H. Kim and C. P. Wilson (eds.), Toward Mental Health of the Rural Elderly. Washington, D. C.:   University Press of America, 1981.   Pp. 205-218.

A discussion of current research on the rural elderly and research which still needs to be done. Notes the 3 kinds of work that social scientists do for the rural aged - working directly with clients in a helping relationship, administration of service programs, and research.

682.   Lassey, William R., and Marie L. Lassey.   "Physical and Mental Health of the Rural Elderly: An Integrated Framework for Research."   Paper presented at the Annual Meeting of the Rural Sociological Society (Ithaca, New York; August, 1980).

Proposes a framework for research with the rural elderly. The authors outline a comparative study examining health service systems of six states through inerviews with 992 elderly people.

683.   Lassey, William R., Marie L. Lassey, Gary R. Lee, and Naomi Lee.   "Research Priorities Concerning the Rural Elderly."   Paper presented at a conference on Research and Public Service with the Rural Elderly at the Western Rural Development Center, Oregon State University (Corvallis, Oregon; October, 1980).

Argues for better research and service delivery for the rural elderly. Points out the absence of research-based knowledge available to practitioners.

684.   Lawton, M. Powell.   "The Elderly in Low Density Areas: Future Environmental Research Needs and Methods."   In Robert C. Atchley with Thomas O. Byerts (eds.), Rural Environments and Aging. Washington, D. C.:   Gerontological Society, 1975. Pp. 257-261.

Suggests possible directions for future research.

Stresses the importance of relating environment to personal dimensions.

685. Lee, Gary R., and Marie L. Lassey. "The Elderly." Paper presented at the Annual Meeting of the Rural Sociological Society (Ithaca, New York; August, 1980).

Reviews previous research on the rural elderly and outlines present research needs of policy planners. Covers topics such as income, health, housing, transportation, and life satisfaction. Many of the questions concerning research needs focus on the increased migration of elderly into rural areas.

686. Madden, J. Patrick. "An Economist's Reaction to the Conference." In Robert C. Atchley with Thomas O. Byerts (eds.), Rural Environments and Aging. Washington, D. C.: Gerontological Society, 1975. Pp. 229-233.

Contends that there is a pervasive lack of concern for validity among the papers presented in Atchley's and Byerts' Rural Environments and Aging. Also notes the lack of a theoretical framework in many of the papers.

687. Moe, Edward O. "Research With the Rural Elderly: A National Perspective." Paper presented at a Conference on Research and Public Service With the Rural Elderly at the Western Rural Development Center, Oregon State University, (Corvallis, Oregon; October, 1980).

Examines goals for older Americans, current research on the elderly, and suggestions for future research. Moe suggests a conceptual framework for categorizing ongoing rural elderly research projects and critiques the general manner in which research is produced and supposedly disseminated to practitioners.

688. Nowak, Carol A. See entry number 348.

689. Shelley, Robert K., and Susan Rodgers Siregar. "Research approaches to the rural elderly: combining survey and ethnographic methodology." Athens, Ohio: Ohio University, 1981.

690. Wilkinson, Carroll Wetzel. See entry number 179.

RETIREMENT

691. Alleger, Daniel E. "The Role of Agriculture in Retirement Adjustment: A Study in Five Florida Counties." Rural Sociology, 20(2):125-131 (June, 1955).

Examines adjustment to retirement among older farmers living in Florida. Covers motives for retirement,

retirement income, and levels of living. The author concludes that agricultural retirees have certain economic and cultural advantages but that these change with increasing age.

692. Bauder, Ward W. "Farmer's Definition of Retirement." The Gerontologist, 7(3):207-212 (September, 1967).

Uses interviews with 575 South Dakota farm operators to explore their definitions of retirement. Discusses labor and management components of farming and how they change as the farmer ages.

693. Bice, Thomas W., and Robert L. Eichhorn. "When Hard Workers Retire." Rural Sociology, 33(4):480-483 (December, 1968).

This short article investigates the relationship between work orientation and retirement decisions, expectations, and satisfaction for a small group of older Indiana farmers. Retired farmers who were rated as higher in work orientation were found to be less satisfied with retirement and more likely to continue working in retirement than low work-oriented farmers.

694. Drake, Joseph T. "The retirement of aged farm owners - factors which inhibit farm owner retirement and a proposed solution." (Doctoral dissertation, University of North Carolina, Chapel Hill, North Carolina, 1951.) Dissertation Abstracts International, 1951, p.216.

695. Farace, Bettie Fisher. "Factors predicting retirement decision-making for Michigan farm families." (Doctoral dissertation, Sociology, Individual and Family Studies, Michigan State University of Agriculture and Applied Science, East Lansing, Michigan, 1978.) Dissertation Abstracts International, 40, 2, A, p.1102.

A study of the factors affecting the decision of when to retire for a sample of 100 Michigan farm families. Degree of work orientation, health of family members, biological changes brought on by aging, and the children's interest in the farm were found to be the primary factors in retirement decision-making.

696. Goudy, Willis J., et. al. "Work and retirement patterns in small towns." Ames, Iowa: Iowa State University, Department of Sociology, 1976.

697. Goudy, Willis J., Sandra C. Burke, E. A. Powers, and P. M. Keith. "Job Deprivation Among Older Farmers." Paper presented at the Annual Meeting of the Rural Sociological Society of America (San Francisco, California; September, 1982).

Examines retiree's feeling of missing work and factors

related to that feeling with data from 1964 and 1974 interviews of Iowa farmers. Retired farmers do not report as much job deprivation as the expected by full time farmers.

698. Hampe, Gary D. See entry number 740.

699. Keating, Norah, and Judith Marshall. "The Process of Retirement: The Rural Self Employed." The Gerontologist, 20(4):437-443 (1980).

Notes the distinction between retirement as an ongoing process rather than a single event for 50 rural couples.

700. Kim, Paul K. H. See entry number 151.

701. Kivett, Vira R., Jean P. Scott, and R. Max Learner. "The Farmer in Later Life: His Status and His Needs." Research and Farming. Raleigh, North Carolina: Agricultural Reseach Station, 38:6-14 (Summer/Autumn) 1978.

702. Lozier, John, and Ronald Althouse. "Retirement to the Porch in Rural Appalachia." International Journal of Aging and Human Development, 6:7-15 (1975).

The authors describe the use of the front porch as a cultural process which allows the elderly, especially males, to maintain a public presence and to continue an active social exchange. The porch facilitates the assertion of claims developed during the lifetime of the elderly person. The porch also acts to enforce the obligation of juniors to provide reciprocity. The process serves to define help to an elder as his due rather than charity.

703. Powers, Edward A., Patricia M. Keith, and Willis J. Goudy. "Later life transitions: older males in rural America." Sociology Report #139. Ames, Iowa: Iowa State University, Sociological Studies in Aging, Department of Sociology and Anthropology, November, 1977.

This report presents findings from longitudinal study of later life patterns of men from non-metropolitan Iowa. Various sections of the report cover topics such as: employment behavior, job attitudes and work values, income, health, and social networks.

704. Sherman S. See entry number 325.

705. Taietz, Philip, Gordon D. Streib, and Milton L. Barron. "Adjustment to Retirement in Rural New York State." Bulletin #919. Ithaca, New York: Cornell Agricultural Experiment Station, (February) 1956.

706. United States House. See entry number 89.

707. United States House. See entry number 90.

708. United States House. See entry number 91.

709. United States Senate. See entry number 92.

710. Wang, Ching-Li. See entry number 57.

711. Wilkinson, Carroll Wetzel. See entry number 178.

712. Wilkinson, Carroll Wetzel. See entry number 179.

713. Youmans, E. Grant. See entry number 796.

RURAL/URBAN DIFFERENCES

714. Ahearn, Mary C. "Health Care in Rural America. Economics, Statistics, and Cooperative Service." _Information Bulletin #428_. Washington, D. C.: United States Department of Agriculture, 1979.

   Discusses rural and urban health needs and resources. Presents demographic health statistics for the elderly. Findings indicate poorer health care systems in rural areas.

715. Aizenberg, Rhonda. See entry number 33.

716. Arling, Greg. See entry number 854.

717. Atchley, Robert C. See entry number 292.

718. Auerbach, Arnold J. "The Elderly in Rural Areas: Differences in Urban Areas and Implications for Practice." In L. H. Ginsberg (ed.), _Social Work in Rural Communities_. New York, New York: Council on Social Work Education, 1976. Pp. 99-107.

   Presents the findings from a 1973 study done in a five-county rural area of southern Illinois outlining problems facing the rural elderly in areas such as transportation, health, isolation, employment, and housing. Compares those findings with results from a Chicago study. Makes suggestions for improving the quality of services to the rural aged.

719. Bastida, Elena. See entry number 408.

720. Bauder, Ward W., and Jon A. Doerflinger. "Work Roles Among the Rural Aged." In E. Grant Youmans (ed.), _Older Rural Americans_. Lexington, Kentucky: University of Kentucky Press, 1967. Pp. 22-43.

   Examines rural-urban differences in work roles, labor force participation of older people, patterns in re-

tirement, and adjustment to retirement. Relies heavily on data from the 1960 census.

721. Berardo, Felix. "Social Adaptation to Widowhood Among
a Rural-Urban Aged Population." Bulletin #689. Pullman,
Washington: Washington Agricultural Experiment Station,
Washington State University, 1967.

722. Berry, C. G., and F. S. Stinson. Service Consumption
Patterns and Service Priorities of the Elderly. Washington,
D. C.: Administration on Aging, Department of Health, Edu-
cation, and Welfare, June, 1977.

    This report presents data from both service providers
    (n=185) and elderly service consumers (n=751) in urban
    and rural areas. Discusses the elderly's actual and
    desired use of services as well as their unmet service
    needs.

723. Blake, Brian F. See entry number 374.

724. Brown, David L. "Health Status Among Low-Income Elderly Persons: Rural-Urban Differences." Social Security Bulletin, 41:14-25 (June, 1978).

    Health status among rural and urban low income elderly
    is explored. Data are from a 1973 national survey by
    the Social Security Administration. Higher rates of
    health disorders are found among rural elderly.

727. Bultena, Gordon. L. "Rural-Urban Differences in the
Familial Interaction of the Aged." Rural Sociology, 34(1):
5-15 (1969).

    Assesses the social isolation of elderly in rural and
    urban communities in Wisconsin. Findings do not sup-
    port the generally accepted hypothesis of greater iso-
    lation among urban aged. An important factor affect-
    ing this finding is the greater out-migration of child-
    ren in rural areas. Author suggests that the deterior-
    ation of family ties is emerging as a more serious pro-
    blem in rural areas than in urban areas.

726. Bylund, Robert A. "A rural-urban comparison of the
housing quality of elderly Americans in 1975." (Doctoral
dissertation, Pennsylvania State University, Sociology, Public and Social Welfare Department, 1979.) Dissertation
Abstracts International, 40, 9, A, p.5208.

    Explores the relationship of rural-urban residence and
    race to housing quality. Describes housing quality of
    the elderly. Lower housing quality was found among the
    elderly with the following characteristics: black,
    poor, rural, less educated, and renting.

727. Bylund, Robert A., Charles O. Crawford, and Nelson L.

LeRay. "Housing Quality of the Elderly: A Rural-Urban Comparison." Journal of Minority Aging, 4:14-24 (1979).

>Examines quality of housing of dwellings headed by per-
>sons 65 or older using 1975 Annual Housing Survey data.
>The authors develop several indicators of housing qual-
>ity and found that quality of housing was positively
>related to size of place.

728. Bylund, Robert A., Nelson L. LeRay, and Charles O. Crawford. "Older American households and their housing 1975: A
metro-nonmetro comparison." University Park, Pennsylvania:
Department of Agricultural Economics and Rural Sociology,
Agricultural Experiment Station, Pennsylvania State University, January, 1980.

>Uses data from the 1975 Annual Housing Survey to com-
>pare metropolitan and nonmetropolitan elderly house-
>holds on selected characteristics of household heads,
>housing units, and housing costs. Nonmetropolitan
>rural elderly household, especially renter households,
>were found to have lower levels of housing, food,
>transportation, clothing, and health care.

729. Clemente, Frank. See entry number 24.

730. Clifford, William B., Tim Heaton, and Glenn V. Fuguitt.
"Residential Mobility and Living Arrangements Among the Elderly: Changing Patterns in Metropolitan and Nonmetropolitan
Areas." International Journal of Aging and Human Development,
14:139-156 (1981-82).

>A descriptive study exploring the relationship between
>living arrangements and residential mobility between
>the 1960's and 1970's using data from the Public Use
>Samples and Current Population Survey. Mobility, par-
>ticularly out-migration from nonmetropolitan areas, was
>greater for the elderly with more dependent living
>arrangements.

731. Costello, T. Patrick, Richard C. Pugh, Bruce F. Stead-
man, and Rosalie, A. Kane. "Perceptions of Urban Versus
Rural Hospital Patients About Return to Their Communities."
Journal of the American Geriatrics Society, 25(12):552-555
(1977).

>Reports findings from interviews with 91 Veterans Ad-
>ministration Hospital patients over 55 years of age
>(48 urban, 43 rural). Rural respondents indicated
>they expected more social interaction and support when
>they returned home. The authors provide some inter-
>esting comments on health care service provision in
>rural areas.

732. D'Elia, Gabrielle. See entry number 205.

733. DeShane, Michael Robert. "The effects of urban-rural
life histories of the aged on urban adaptation." (Doctoral
dissertation, Portand State University, Portland, Oregon, 19-
77.) Dissertation Abstracts International, 38, 6, A.

>   This study investigates the impact of residential his-
>   tory on the adaptation of the elderly living in urban
>   settings by comparing elderly who were raised in rural
>   versus urban places. The hypotheses tested are derived
>   from Wirth's work on the impact of city living on per-
>   sonality and behavior. Partial support for Wirth's
>   ideas is forthcoming.

734. Donnenwerth, Gregory V. See entry number 379.

735. Douglas, Barbara. See entry number 340.

736. Ellenbogen, Bert L. "Health Status of the Rural Aged."
In E. Grant Youmans (ed.), Older Rural Americans. Lexington,
Kentucky: University of Kentucky Press, 1967. Pp. 195-220.

>   Presents data on the health of the rural aged compared
>   with the urban elderly using 1960-65 data from HEW
>   and Vital Statistics. The data indicate that the rural
>   elderly have: lower health status, fewer health re-
>   sources, but improving health levels.

737. Fuguitt, Glenn V. See entry number 36.

738. Goldstein, Sidney. "Urban and Rural Differentials in
Consumer Patterns of the Aged, 1960-1961." Rural Sociology,
31:333-345 (1966).

>   Analyzes 1960 data to discover the impact of residence
>   on the elderly's income, expenditures, and savings.
>   Urban elderly households were considerably higher on
>   these measures than rural ones.

739. Grams, Armin. See entry number 548.

740. Hampe, Gary D., Audie L. Elevins, Jr., and Sheila Nyhus.
"The Influence of Rural-Urban Residence and Perceptions of
Health on Retirement Satisfaction." Paper presented at the
32nd Annual Meeting of the Gerontological Society of America
(Washington, D. C.; November, 1979).

>   Examines the interrelationships between the rural-urban
>   variable and self-percieved physical and mental health
>   in relation to retirement satisfaction with data from
>   interviews of 744 retired persons from Wyoming. While
>   retirement satisfaction was positively associated with
>   health attitudes, it was not associated with place of
>   residence.

741. Harootyan, Robert. See entry number 447.

742. Hynson, Lawrence M., Jr. "Rural-Urban Differences in Satisfaction Among the Elderly." Rural Sociology, 40:64-66 (Spring, 1975).

    Examines differences in satisfaction among rural and urban elderly in the areas of family, community, self, and others with data from a 1973 national survey. The urban elderly reported lower levels of satisfaction with their community, more fear in general, and less general happiness than their rural counterparts.

743. Hynson, Lawrence M., Jr. "A Further Note on Elderly, Satisfaction, and Place of Residence." Rural Sociology, 42: 108-109 (Spring, 1977).

    A commentary responding to criticisms by Sauer, Shehan, and Boymel (1976) of author's study on differences in rural and urban satisfaction among the elderly. States that the re-analysis of his original study suffers from several methodological weaknesses.

744. Kaplan, Jerome. See entry number 565.

745. Key, William H. "Rural-Urban Differences and the Family." The Sociological Quarterly, 2:49-56 (1961).

    Reports work on a scale of social participation by which comparisons of interaction patterns of rural and urban dwellers can be made. Authors developed scales originated by Queen and by Barnard. Findings do not support the tested hypothesis, i.e., the disintegration of the family in urban areas.

746. Kim, Paul K. H. See entry number 151.

747. Kivett, Vira R. See entry number 449.

748. Klemer, R. H., et. al. "The North Carolina Rural Aged." Springfield, Virginia: United States Department of Commerce, National Technical Information Service, 1975.

    A report on the characteristics of North Carolina's rural and urban aged.

749. Kreps, Juanita M. "Economic Status of the Rural Aged." In E. Grant Youmans (ed.), Older Rural Americans. Lexington, Kentucky: University of Kentucky Press, 1967. Pp. 144-168.

    Reports on the economic status of the rural versus urban elderly using data from the early 1960's. The rural elderly have significantly lower incomes than the urban elderly but also a lower cost of living.

750. Krout, John A. See entry number 578.

751. Kwan, Yui-huen, et. al. "Residence as a Factor in Lon-

gevity: A Study of Louisianians on the Differences in Aging
of Persons Living in Rural and Urban Areas." Proceedings of
the Rural Sociology Section of the Southern Association of
Agricultural Science, 1977.

752. Kwan, Yui-huen, and Alvin L. Bertrand. "Mortality and
Longevity in Louisiana: The Relationship of Rural Residence
to Survival After Age 65." Louisiana State University, Bulletin #707. Baton Rouge, Louisiana: Center for Agricultural
Sciences and Rural Development, 1978.

> Examines the effect of rural-urban residence on longe-
> vity after the age of 65. Subjects were all Louisiana
> residents 65 and over who died or survived during the
> period from 1962-1974.

753. Laurie, W., and William M. Shook, Jr. "Urban and Rural
Older People: Their Well-Being and Needs." Paper presented
at the Annual Meeting of the Rural Sociological Society (San
Diego, California; November, 1980).

> Presents findings from a comparative analysis of the
> well-being and needs of samples of rural and urban el-
> derly living in Ohio, Oregon, and Kentucky. The rural
> Kentucky elderly were found to be worse off in terms of
> health, security, loneliness, and outlook on life. The
> magnitude of unmet need in all locations was substantial.

754. Lee, Gary R. "Rural-Urban Residence and Emotional Well-
Being Among the Elderly." Paper presented at the Annual Meeting of the Rural Sociological Society (Guelph, Canada; August,
1981).

> Explores the effect of rural/urban residence on sub-
> jective well-being. One thousand, six hundred sixty
> five (1665) adults, 65 and older, residing in the state
> of Washington responded to mailed questionnaires. The
> data indicated very small differences between the rural
> and urban elderly.

755. Lee, Gary R. "Residential Location and Fear of Crime
Among the Elderly." Rural Sociology, 47(4):655-669 (1982).

> Using survey data from a sample of aged 55 and over
> Washington state residents, this research examines the
> relationship between residential location (measured by
> an 8 point continuum) and fear of crime. The findings
> indicate that fear of crime does not increase linearly
> with size of place of residence and that sex is an im-
> portant qualifier of the size of place/fear of crime
> relationship.

756. Lee Gary R., and Marie L. Lassey. "Residence and Aging:
Directions for Future Research." Paper presented at the An-
nual Meeting of the Rural Sociological Society (Burlington,
Vermont; August, 1979).

Discusses the paradox found in much of the literature on rural-urban differences in subjective well-being of the elderly. Although disadvantaged in objective conditions, the rural elderly are often found to express higher levels of subjective well-being.

757. Lee, Gary R., and Marie L. Lassey. "Rural-Urban Differences Among the Elderly: Economic, Social, and Subjective Factors." Journal of Social Issues, 36:62-74 (Spring, 1980).

The authors argue that although research has cosistently shown objective quality of life for the rural elderly to be lower than that of the urban elderly, there has been no such consistency among research on the subjective quality of life.

758. Lee, Gary R., and Marie L. Lassey. "Rural-Urban Residence and Aging: Directions for Future Research." Paper presented at a conference on Research and Public Service with the Rural Elderly at the Western Rural Development Center, Oregon State University (Corvallis, Oregon; October, 1980).

Reviews previous research on differences between the rural and urban elderly in subjective well-being and suggests ways in which the question of such differences could be better examined.

759. Lowe, George D., and Charles W. Peek. "Location and Lifestyle: The Comparative Explanatory Ability of Urbanism and Rurality." Rural Sociology, 39:393-420 (Fall, 1974).

Data are drawn from interviews of three samples of United States adults taken by the Gallop organization. The rural-urban variable is conceptualized as both lifestyle and location. Drinking of alcoholic beverages is used as the indicator of rural-urban lifestyles. The addition of this lifestyle indicator greatly increased the predictive capabilities of the rural-urban variable.

760. McCoy, John L., and David L. Brown. "Health Status Among Low-Income Elderly Persons: Rural/Urban Differences." Social Security Bulletin, 41(6):14-26 (June, 1978).

A statistical comparison of the health status of rural versus urban elderly. The greatest number of health problems were found among the elderly living in the most rural places.

761. McKain, Walter C., Jr. "Aging and Rural Life." In W. Donahue and C. Tibbits (eds.), The New Frontiers of Aging. Ann Arbor, Michigan: University of Michigan Press, 1957. Pp. 118-128.

Three rural communities and one city in Connecticut

are examined to test the hypothesis that adjustment for older people in rural areas does not differ markedly from that of older people in urban areas.

762. Mahoney, Kevin J. "A National Perspective on Rural-Urban Differences in the Interaction of the Aged With Their Adult Children." The Gerontologist, 17:94 (October, 1977).

Compares quality and quantity of interaction between the aged and their adult children in four types of communities: rural, small town, suburban, and urban. Based on a national sample of 2,797 persons age 65 and older. The urban elderly are less likely to get phys-ical assistance or advice from their off-spring.

763. Maurer, Richard C., James A. Christenson, and Paul D. Warner. "Perspectives of Community Services Among Rural and Urban Elderly." Paper presented at the Annual Meeting of the Rural Sociological Society (Ithaca, New York; August, 1980).

Compares the elderly's perceptions of service problems of the elderly to the perceptions of younger adults and public officials with data from 2 North Carolina statewide citizen surveys, one Kentucky citizen sur-vey, and one Kentucky survey of community officials. The elderly do not see services as any more of a pro-blem then the nonelderly. The effect of residence on community service perceptions was not consistent across the surveys.

764. Miller, Michael K., and Kelly W. Grader. "Rural-Urban Differences in Two Dimensions of Community Satisfaction." Rural Sociology, 44:489-504 (Fall, 1979).

Data were collected in 1972 by means of interviews with 595 residents from five counties in Utah representing three different positions along a hypothetical rural-urban continuum. Two dimensions of community satis-faction (economic and interpersonal) were identified. Urban residents had significantly higher levels of community satisfaction than rural residents.

765. Murphey, Milledge. "Similarities and Dissimilarities in Attitudes Toward Death Among Rural Elderly Populations." Omega, 9(4):(1978-1979).

This article examines the attitudes of 170 Florida elderly towards death. Both rural and urban communi-ties were studied. The rural elderly had more tra-ditional beliefs in the after life.

766. Nahemow, Lucille, and M. Powell Lawton. "Urban-Rural Differences in Adjustment to Housing for the Elderly." Paper presented at the Annual Meeting of the Gerontological Society of America (Dallas, Texas; November, 1978).

Presents findings from a national study on the housing satisfaction of the aged living in rural versus urban public housing units. The authors report greater satisfaction with housing among the rural residents.

767. Nelson, Gary. "Social Services to the Urban and Rural Aged: The Experience of Area Agencies on Aging." The Gerontologist, 20(2):200-207 (April, 1980).

This article analyzes data on the organizational characteristics and capacities, success in mobilizing resources, contextual environments, and service expenditure patterns of 137 Area Agencies on Aging located in rural and urban areas. Rural AAA's were found to be particularly weak in terms of fiscal and professional staff resources necessary for the development of a broad range of care.

768. Nelson, Gary. "A Comparative Analysis of Title XX Services to the Urban and Rural Elderly." Paper presented at the Annual Meeting of the Gerontological Society of America (Toronto, Canada, November, 1981).

Provides policy makers, planners, and administrators in the aging network with comparative findings on the provision of services to the urban and rural elderly under Title XX of the Social Security Act. Data come from a national data base derived from the state Title XX Plans for all states and the District of Columbia (1979-1980).

769. Nowak, Carol A. See entry number 348.

770. Older American Reports. "Rural Poor Elderly Use Fewer Health Services Than Urban Counterparts, Study Shows." Older American Reports, 2(16):(August, 1978).

Cites 1973 data from a Social Security Bulletin indidating that the rural poor elderly have poorer health than the urban elderly but use fewer health services.

771. Richard, Terry Trevino. "A Comparison of Differential Needs Among Rural and Urban Elderly in Two Southeast Arkansas Counties." In Paul K. H. Kim and C. P. Wilson (eds.), Toward Mental Health of the Rural Elderly. Washington, D. C.: University Press of America, 1981. Pp. 187-194.

An analysis of differences between needs and support systems of rural versus urban areas and rural farm versus rural nonfarm. Interviews were conducted in 179 households in two southeast Arkansas counties. Findings did not support the generally accepted contention that the rural elderly are more disadvantaged than urban elderly.

772. Robinson, Ira E., Harold Bronfin, and Jack O. Balswick. "Nursing Home Resources and Rural and Urban Needs." Journal

of Health and Social Behavior, 11:146-151 (June, 1970).

    Examines the relationship between nursing home person-
nel and facilities and needs found in rural and urban
areas with data from 148 licensed nursing homes in Georgia. Surprisingly, the authors found that rural nursing homes have more adequate personnel and facilities.

773. Rosen, Catherine F. See entry number 635.

774. Sauer, William J., Constance Shehan, and Carl Boymel.
"Rural-Urban Differences in Satisfaction Among the Elderly:
A Reconsideration." Rural Sociology, 41:269-275 (Summer,
1976).

    Disputes many of the methods and findings of a 1975
study by Hynson on the relationship between size of
place and several types of satisfaction among the elderly. They claim that Hynson's findings of greater
satisfaction among the rural elderly are not supported
when the data are analyzed by means of multi-variate
statistics.

775. Sauer, William J., Wayne Seelbach, and Sandra Hanson.
"Rural-Urban and Cohort Differences in Filial Responsibility
Norms." Journal of Minority Aging, 5(4):299-305 (1980).

    This paper examines rural-urban differences in filial
responsibility toward elderly parents among a large
sample of Wisconsin residents. Large differences based
on residence are not found.

776. Schooler, Kermit K. "A Comparison of Rural and Non-
Rural Elderly on Selected Variables." In Robert C. Atchley
with Thomas O. Byerts (eds.), Rural Environments and Aging.
Washington, D. C.: Gerontological Society, 1975. Pp. 27-42.

    Describes differences between rural and urban elderly
with data from a national sample of 4,000 U.S. residents
and a follow-up study three years later of a sub-sample
of 521 respondents. Areas examined include: demographics, morale, health, social relationships, and environmental characteristics. The author suggests that
while relatively small differences appear to exist based
on residence, there are greater differences in the process of aging between rural and urban areas.

777. Stafford, Magdalen Marrow. "Self-initiated use of support systems and health services for perceived health needs
by aged persons in metropolitan and nonmetropolitan living
sites." (Doctoral dissertation, Case Western Reserve University, Cleveland, Ohio, September, 1981.) Dissertation Abstracts International, 42, 3, B, p.969B.

    Uses a sample of 60 metropolitan and 60 nonmetropolitan
elderly residents to study the influence of age and

place of residence on the elderly's perception of health needs, use of informal and formal support systems, and use of physician services. The relationships between these sets of variables were found to be significantly affected by place of residence.

778. Taietz, Philip. "The Needs of the Elderly: Rural-Urban Comparisons." Paper presented at a workshop on Rural Gerontology Research in the Northeast at the Northeast Regional Center for Rural Development, Cornell University (Ithaca, New York; May, 1977).

Reviews previous research to compare the needs of rural and urban elderly.

779. Taietz, Philip. "Rural-Urban Differences in the Formal and Informal Support systems." Symposium presented at the Annual Meeting of the Gerontological Society of America (Boston, Massachusetts; November, 1982).

Discusses rural/urban differences on the availability, accessibility, and utilization of a broad range of services for the elderly. Considers issues such as fiscal constraints, staffing, structural complexity, planning and coordination, and community attitudes.

780. Taietz, Philip, and Sande Milton. "Rural-Urban Differences in the Structure of Services for the Elderly in Upstate New York Counties." Journal of Gerontology, 34:429-437(1979).

This paper examines changes in the elderly service structure of 53 upstate New York state counties between 1967 and 1976 with special attention given to rural/urban differences. Among other findings the authors report that services in all places have increased over time, rural/urban differences have decreased, and urban offices for the aging have higher scores of community effectiveness.

781. United States Bureau of the Census. See entry number 53.

782. United States Bureau of the Census. See entry number 54.

783. United States Department of Commerce. See entry number 476.

784. United State House. See entry number 328.

785. Van Es, J. C., and J. E. Brown, Jr. "The Rural-Urban Variable Once More: Some Individual Level Observations." Rural Sociology, 39:373-391 (Fall, 1974).

Assesses the relevance of the rural-urban variable for explaining individual differences in values and behavior with data from interviews of 322 male, white, heads of household from an eleven-county area surrounding Quincy,

Illinois. Socio-economic status was found to be a stronger predictor of several indicators of socio-cultural attitudes and behaviors than occupation or residence.

786. Welichs, K. W., and P. K. Kim. "Differential Needs of the Metropolitan, Small Town and Rural Elderly: Service Implications." The Gerontologist, 15(5):96 (1975).

Disscusses the needs of 150 randomly selected persons residing in three different localities. In person interviews included items on respondents' degree of perceived need and problem areas. All three groups defined social isolation, economic poverty, transportation, and health as most severe problems.

787. Whittington, Frank. "Reaction to 'A Comparison of Rural and Non-Rural Elderly on Selected Variables'." In Robert C. Atchley with Thomas O. Byerts (eds.), Rural Environments and Aging. Washington, D. C.: Gerontological Society, 1975. Pp. 43-46.

Comments on conceptual and methodological issues concerning the paper, "A Comparison of Rural and Non-Rural Elderly on Selected Variables" by Kermit Schooler. Notes the paper's strength as the basis for much future research.

788. Wilkinson, Carroll Wetzel. See entry number 178.

789. Wilkinson, Carroll Wetzel. See entry number 179.

790. Willie, C. V. See entry number 287.

791. Wozny, Mark C., et. al. "Review of Reported Differences Between the Rural and Urban Elderly: Status, Needs, Services, and Service Costs." Washington, D. C.: United States Department of Health, Education, and Welfare, Office of Human Developmental Services, Administration on Aging, 1981.

A comprehensive review of research findings on rural/urban elderly differences. Focuses on basic characteristics, needs assessment, economic resources, service availability and accessibility, and costs of aging services.

792. Ybarra, G. "Assessment of comprehensive home health." Austin, Texas: University of Texas Center for Social Work Research, 1976.

A comparison of an urban and a rural Texas comprehensive home health care program designed to facilitate independent living arrangements for the elderly.

793. Youmans, E. Grant. "Health problems of older persons in selected rural and urban areas of Kentucky." Progress Report

#104. Lexington, Kentucky: University of Kentucky, Agri-
cultural Experiment Station, 1961.

794. Youmans, E. Grant. "Pessimism Among Older Rural and
Urban Persons." Journal of Health and Human Behavior, 2:132-
137 (Summer, 1961).

> Examines pessimism among older rural and urban persons
> and implications for 'the achievement syndrome' with
> data from a 1959 survey in rural and urban Kentucky.
> Greater degrees of pessimism were found for those elder-
> ly who were: male, in poor health, lower socioeconomic
> status, and rural residents.

795. Youmans, E. Grant. "Leisure-time activities of older
persons in selected rural and urban areas of Kentucky." Lexington, Kentucky: Kentucky Agricultural Experiment Station,
1962.

> An examination of the use and perception of leisure time
> among elderly residents of both rural and urban Kentucky
> areas. Small differences were found based on residence
> with the urban elderly reporting a higher level of par-
> ticipation in formal activities and the rural elderly
> reporting higher levels in informal leisure time pur-
> suits.

796. Youmans, E. Grant. "Objective and Subjective Economic
Disengagement Among Older Rural and Urban Men." Journal of
Gerontology, 21:439-441 (1966).

> Using data from a 1959 survey of rural and urban Ken-
> tucky men, this paper examines economic disengagement
> among the elderly and its relationship with residence.
> Those males aged 75 and over in both areas reported
> less involvement in work roles and smaller incomes but
> experienced fewer feelings of economic deprivation.

797. Youmans, E. Grant. "Disengagement Among Older Rural
and Urban Men." In E. Grant Youmans (ed.), Older Rural Americans. Lexington, Kentucky: University of Kentucky Press,
1967. Pp. 97-116.

> Explores disengagement from work, family, hobbies, and
> community involvement with data from 1959 interviews
> of two samples of Kentucky rural and urban men. Com-
> pares those 60-64 with those 75 and older. While
> objective economic disengagement was greater for males
> aged 75 and over, this same group experienced less
> subjective economic deprivation.

798. Youmans, E. Grant. "Family Disengagement Among Older
Urban and Rural Women." Journal of Gerontology, 22:209-211
(1967).

> Examines disengagement from family visiting patterns

and helping relationships for two samples of older women living in urban and rural communities. Data are
obtained from a 1959 survey of older persons in Kentucky.
Findings offer very slight evidence of disengagement and
only in rural areas.

799. Youmans, E. Grant. "Health Orientations of Older Rural
and Urban Men." Geriatrics, 22:139-147 (October, 1967).

Compares two age groups of men, those 60-64 and those
75 and over from rural and urban Kentucky, to determine
the relationship between age, residence, and health
orientations. The data indicate that rural elderly
males have lower levels of physical and mental health
and health orientations than urban males.

800. Youmans, E. Grant. "Generation and Perceptions of Old
Age: An Urban-Rural Comparison." The Gerontologist, 1:284-
288 (Winter, 1971).

Data are from 1969 interviews of 805 men and women living in rural and urban areas of Kentucky. Examines
several questions: How do perceptions of old age differ between generations? How does residence influence
generational differences? What are the implications
of the differnces?

801. Youmans, E. Grant. Social Aspects of Aging in Appalachia. Springfield, Virginia: National Technical Information
Service, United States Department of Commerce, 1971.

A comparison of rural and urban elderly on social adjustment and disengagement.

802. Youmans, E. Grant. "Age group and attitudes: an urban-
rural comparison." Lexington, Kentucky: University of Kentucky, Department of Sociology, 1974.

This manuscript compares different age groups living in
rural and urban Kentucky on the following: attitudes,
self-image, morale, family life, economic conditions,
and community life. Attitudes were found to become less
favorable with age for both the urban and rural aged.

803. Youmans, E. Grant. "Age Group, Health, and Attitudes."
The Gerontologist, 14(3):249-254 (1974).

A study of the ways in which four age groups (20-29,
30-44, 45-59, and 60 and over) differ on perceived
health status and attitudinal reactions to their health
conditions. The data are collected from 803 men and
women living in a rural county in the Southern Appalachian Region and in a metropolitan central city. Urban
respondents in all groups reported more health problems.

804. Youmans, E. Grant. See entry number 183.

805. Youmans, E. Grant. "Attitudes: Young-Old and Old-Old." The Gerontologist, 17(2):175-178 (April, 1977).

 Compares attitude scale scores for 224 persons aged 55-74 and 42 persons aged 75 and over living in a rural and urban community. Substantial age differences were found for the urban residents but not for rural dwellers.

SOCIAL CHANGE

806. Britton, Joseph H., William G. Mather, and Alice K. Lansing. "Expectations for Older Persons in a Rural Community: Community Participation." Rural Sociology, 27:387-395 (December, 1962).

 Interviewed one adult in each of 487 households in a rural Pennsylvania community. Examines social norms as they concern expectations about older persons' participation in community affairs.

807. Clemente, Frank, and Richard S. Krannich. "Industrial Development and the Rural Aged." In Paul K. H. Kim and C. P. Wilson (eds.), Toward Mental Health of the Rural Elderly. Washington, D. C.: University Press of America, 1981. Pp. 117-126.

 Argues that in the United States today there is a strong trend toward industrial development of small communities and this results in a decline in the economic status of the elderly in the area. Data are from a longitudinal study conducted in an experimental and a control region in Illinois. Findings strongly support the authors' hypothesis.

808. Clemente, Frank, and Gene F. Summers. "Industrial Development and the Elderly: A Longitudinal Analysis." Journal of Gerontology, 28(4):479-483 (1973).

 Explores the impact of industrial development upon the rural elderly. Data are from two groups in Illinois: one near a recently built manufacturing facility and one from a control region across the state. Findings show a negative impact on the economic status of the elderly resulting from industrial development.

809. Davenport, Joseph, and Judith A. Davenport. "Boom Towns and the Aged: Problems and Promises in Cowboy Country." In Paul K. H. Kim and C. P. Wilson (eds.), Toward Mental Health of the Rural Elderly. Washington, D. C.: University Press of America, 1981. Pp. 317-328.

 Explores the effect of rapid energy development on the elderly in small towns and rural areas. Resulting problems for the aged include increased housing and energy costs, overload on human service systems, and social structural changes to the community.

810. Fennell, Valerie, I. "Age Relations and Rapid Change in a Small Town." The Gerontologist, 17(5):405-411 (October, 1977).

    A study of the reactions of young and middle-aged adults versus aged adults to sudden economic growth in a small town. Adopts what the author calls a ho-listic anthropological perspective. Also compares long time community residents with more recent in migrants.

811. Larson, S. S. "The Elderly: Victims of the Energy Venture." In Joseph Davenport III and Judith Ann Davenport (eds.), The Boom Town: Problems and Promises in the Energy Vortex. Laramie, Wyoming: University of Wyoming, 1980.

812. Wershow, Harold J. "Days Beyond Recall: Subsistence Homesteading in the Rural South: Circa 1920." International Journal of Aging and Human Development, 6:1-5 (1975).

SOCIAL PARTICIPATION

813. Goudy Willis J. See entry number 382.

814. McKain, Walter C. See entry number 367.

815. Mayo, Selz C. "Age Profiles of Social Participation in Rural Areas of Wake County, North Carolina." Rural Sociology, 15:242-251 (1950).

    Examines the relationship between age and participation of rural people in formal organizations for a sample of 1,400 elderly. Older age groups report lower scores of social participation.

816. Mayo, Selz C. "Social Participation Among the Older Population in Rural Areas of Wake County, North Carolina." Social Forces, 30:53-59 (1951).

817. Pihlblad, C. Terence. See entry number 397.

818. Powers, R. C., et. al. "Study of the Patterns of Liv-ing of the Elderly in Iowa Non-Urban Population Centers." Bulletin #65. Ames, Iowa: Home Economics Research Institute, University of Iowa, 1971.

    Analyzes the living patterns of elderly residents of rural Iowa. The authors argue that the data do not support the thesis that the rural elderly are isolated.

819. Rosencranz, H. A., et. al. "Social participation of older people in the small town." Columbia, Missouri: De-partment of Sociology, University of Missouri, 1968.

820. Smith, Stanley H. "Reaction of Culture, Life-Style, and Social Environments of the Small Town." In Robert C.

Atchley with Thomas O. Byerts (eds.), <u>Rural Environments and Aging</u>. Washington, D C.: Gerontological Society, 1975. Pp. 63-66.

> Discusses the paper, "Culture, Life-Style, and Social Environment of the Small Town" by C. T. Pihlblad. Notes its discursive, descriptive nature.

821. Taietz, Philip, and Olaf F. Larson. "Social Participation and Old Age." <u>Rural Sociology</u>, 21(3-4):229 (September-December, 1956).

> This study examines the relationship between social participation and old age among 417 residents of four rural New York state communities. Low formal organization participation was found for low status rural males. Age was less strongly related to reduced participation than either socio-economic status or retirement.

TRANSPORTATION AND MOBILITY

822. American University. <u>Conferences on Transportation Needs in the 70's</u>. Springfield, Virginia: National Technical Information Service, 1972.

823. Burkhardt, Jon E. "Transportation and the Rural Elderly." In E. J. Cantilli and June L. Schmelzer (eds.), <u>Transportation and Aging: Selected Issues</u>. Washington, D. C.: United States Government Printing Office, 1970. Pp. 162-166.

> Describes the results of an experimental West Virginia program in which free bus service was provided for the rural elderly. Predictably, the author reports that the number of social and recreational trips by the elderly increased as a result of the program.

824. Burkhardt, Jon E. "Review of 'Transportation of the Rural Aged.'" In Robert C. Atchley with Thomas O. Byerts (eds.), <u>Rural Environments and Aging</u>. Washington, D. C.: Gerontological Society, 1975. Pp. 217-222.

> Argues that Fred Cottrell's pessimism regarding the transportation problems of the rural elderly is unwarranted. Some good rural transportation systems exist.

825. Cantilli, E. J., and June L. Schmelzer (eds.). <u>Transportation and Aging: Selected Issues</u>. Washington, D. C.: United States Government Printing Office, 1970.

826. Cleland, Courtney B. "Mobility of Older People." In Arnold M. Rose and Warren A. Peterson (eds.), <u>Older People and Their Social World</u>. Philadelphia, Pennsylvania: F. A. Davis Co., 1965. Pp. 323-339.

Interviews of 109 aged residents of Northwood, North
Dakota provide the data for this study. Reviews available research on the mobility of older people and outlines areas in need of further research and theoretical
development. Also reports data from a study of a small
community with 25% of its population age 65 and over.

827. Cottrell, Fred. "Transportation of Older People in a
Rural Community." Sociological Focus, 5:29-40 (1971-72).

Examines the effect of a free transportation service
on the elderly of a rural Ohio county. Approximately
50% of the elderly used the service with use greatest
for females, those over age 70, and those living alone.
The author argues that such a service can help the
elderly maintain their independence and living in the
community.

828. Cottrell, Fred. "Transportation of the Rural Aged."
In Robert C. Atchley with Thomas O. Byerts (eds.), Rural
Environments and Aging. Washington, D. C.: Gerontological
Society, 1975. Pp. 187-216.

A summary of existing knowledge about transportation
of the rural elderly. The limited literature available
indicates a considerable lack of transportation for
the elderly.

829. Cutler, Stephen J. "The Availability of Personal Transportation, Residential Location, and Life Satisfaction Among
the Aged." Journal of Gerontology, 27:383-389 (1972).

Explores the relationship between the availability of
personal transportation and life satisfaction of the
elderly with data from a 1970 survey in which interviews were conducted in a community of approximately
9,000. The data do not support the hypothesis that
availability of transportation is related to life
satisfaction.

830. Doeksen, Gerald A. See entry number 244.

831. Doeksen, Gerald A., Shew-Eng H. Webb, Barbara Broeckel-
man, and Robert Carroll. "The Economics of Providing Transportation for the Elderly in Rural Oklahoma." Oklahoma Current Farm Economics. (Oklahoma State University, Agricultural Experiment Station), 53(1):22-31 (March, 1980).

832. Gombeski, William Robert, Jr. See entry number 251.

833. Kaye, I. "Transportation Problems of the Older American in Rural Areas." Rural Development. Washington, D. C.:
United States Senate Report on Agriculture and Forestry,
1972.

834. Kaye, I. "The Brass Ring in the Golden Years." Per-

spective on Aging, 30-32 (January/February, 1978).

> Discusses the high cost and lack of transportation for
> a large percentage of rural elderly. Describes several
> states' attempts to meet transportation needs.

835. Kim, Paul K. H. See entry number 151.

836. Larson, Donald K. See entry number 456.

837. Levy, Steve, K. William Easter, Harold Jansen, and
Jerry Fruin. "Planning Transportation Systems for Older
Rural Americans." Bulletin #519. St. Paul, Minnesota: Uni-
versity of Minnesota, Agricultural Experiment Station, 1977.

838. McKelvey, Douglas J. "Planning and operating transportation systems for older Americans...in rural areas." Iowa
City, Iowa: University of Iowa, Institute of Urban and Regional Research, 1975.

839. McKelvey, Douglas J. "Transportation Issues and Problems of the Rural Elderly." In S. M. Golant (ed.), Location and Environment of Elderly Population. Washington, D.
C.: V. H. Winston & Sons, 1979. Pp. 135-140.

> This chapter identifies some of the basic aspects of
> the transportation problems facing the rural elderly.
> The author cites a lack and inefficency of alternatives
> to the private automobile as major issues and outlines
> crucial transportation questions that need to be ad-
> dressed.

840. McKelvey, D. J., et. al. Transportation planning:
the urban and rural interface and transit needs of the rural
elderly." Iowa City, Iowa: University of Iowa, Institute
of Urban and Regional Research, August, 1974.

841. New York Senate Research Service. See entry number 466.

842. Notess, C. B. "Rural Elderly Transit Markets." American Institute of Planning Journal, 44:328-334 (July, 1978).

> In this article the author argues that the transporta-
> tion demand of the rural elderly can be estimated us-
> ing a number of data sources.

843. Notess, C., et. al. Transportation of Elderly to Rural
Social Services. Blacksburg, Virginia: Center for Urban
and Regional Studies, August, 1975.

844. Orr, Robert H. "The need for transportation services
among rural elderly." Tennessee Farm and Home Science
Progress Report #105. Eastern Tennessee: Tennessee Agricultural Experiment Station, 1978. Pp. 16-18.

> Reports data on the transportation needs of a sample of

1,003 elderly persons living in rural Tennessee. More
than one-third of those surveyed stated that lack of
transportation prevented them from doing necessary
tasks. Despite such need, over 80 percent did not know
of existing transportation services.

845. Patton, Carl Vernon. "Age Groupings and Travel in a
Rural Area." Rural Sociology, 40:55-63 (Spring, 1975).

Focuses on trip-making behavior of older rural persons,
specifically frequency of trips, their purpose, and
mode of travel. Data were collected via 335 questionnaires mailed to residents of Hillsboro, Illinois.
Over 80 percent of the elderly respondents made at
least one trip per day with women and the old-old making trips less frequently.

846. Patton, Carl Vernon, William C. Lienesch, and James R.
Anderson. "Busing the Rural Elderly." Traffic Quarterly,
81-97 (January, 1975).

Describes a successful minibus program serving over
200 rural elderly people in south, central Illinois.
The authors found that the free minibus service had
the following effects on the rural elderly: increased
the length and frequency of their trips, increased the
number of elderly making trips, and had a positive
affect on their attitudes about their community life.

847. Radke, Charleen. "Transportation and the Elderly Mon-
tanan." Generations (Western Gerontological Society), Fall:
22-23 (1977).

A brief description of Montana's use of funds provided
through the Urban Mass Transportation Act to purchase
vehicles to serve the transportation needs of the
elderly. Presents a short discussion on the Section
16 (b)(2) program from which the funds were obtained.

848. Transportation Research Board. Transportation for the
Elderly, Disadvantaged, and Handicapped People in Rural Areas.
Washington, D. C.: Transportation Research Board, 1976.

849. United States Senate. Agriculture and Forestry Committee. Transportation of People in Rural Areas: Rural
Transit Needs, Operations, and Management. (Prepared for the
Subcommittee on Rural Development) (93rd Congress, 1st Session.) Washington, D. C.: United States Government Printing Office, 1974.

850. Wilkinson, Carroll Wetzel. See entry number 178.

851. Wilkinson, Carroll Wetzel. See entry number 179.

852. Wozny, M. C., R. J. Bamberger, and J. S. Revis. "Trans-

portation Services for Older Americans." Paper presented at
the Annual Meeting of the Gerontological Society of America
(Toronto, Canada; November, 1981).

> Reviews the findings of an AoA study evaluating the
> current status of transportation services to the elder-
> ly and identifying problems experienced by service pro-
> viders. Based on telephone interviews with 102 AAAs
> and 60 transportation providers and field visits to
> 20 projects.

853. Youmans, E. Grant, et. al. "Social Adjustment of Rural
Aged in Eastern Kentucky." Paper presented at the Annual
Meeting of the Gerontological Society (San Juan, Puerto Rico;
1972).

WIDOWHOOD

854. Arling, Greg. "Resistance to Isolation Among Elderly
Widows." International Journal of Aging and Human Development, 7(1):67-86 (1976).

> Rural/urban study of black and white widows from the
> Peidmont region of South Carolina. Surveyed 409 widows,
> age 65 and older. Good health and available economic
> resources are primary factors facilitating involvement
> in diverse daily activities with friends, family, and
> neighbors. Higher education was also a factor.

855. Berardo, Felix. See entry number 721.

856. Douglas, Barbara. See entry number 340.

857. Heyman, D. K., et. al. "Long Term Adaption by the
Elderly to Bereavement." Journal of Gerontology, 28(3):356-
362 (1973).

> This article examines the elderly's adaption to the
> death of a spouse among a sample of 258 rural elderly
> persons. Psychological profiles indicate the elderly
> did adapt successfully.

858. Jolley, J. See entry number 386.

859. Kivett, Vira R. "Loneliness and the Rural Widow." The
Family Coordinator, 27:389-394 (October, 1978).

> Reports data on loneliness among 103 rural elderly
> widows. Approximately 25 percent of the respondents
> reported being lonely quite often or never lonely.
> The remaining 50 percent reported being lonely some-
> times.

860. Scott, Jean Pearson, and Vira R. Kivett. "The Widowed

Black Older Adult in the Rural South: Implications for Policy." _Family Relations_, 29:83-90 (January, 1980).

> This article presents data on the needs of 72 widowed rural elderly North Carolina blacks. They were found to be more disadvantaged than the larger sample from which the data was taken.

861. Wilkinson, Carroll Wetzel. See entry number 178.

862. Wilkinson, Carroll Wetzel. See entry number 179.

WOMEN

863. Brown, P. T. See entry number 494.

864. Hooyman, Nancy R. See entry number 345.

865. Hooyman, Nancy R. See entry number 346.

866. Jolley, J. See entry number 386.

867. Kivett, Vira R. "Older Rural Displaced Homemakers: Perspectives on Status and Morale." Paper presented at the Annual Meeting of the Gerontological Society of America (Toronto, Canada; November, 1981).

> This paper presents data on the characteristics, needs, and morale of a small sample (n-84) of older rural women who were either widowed or divorced and had not previously held major work roles outside the home. High levels of dependency in housing and transportation were found among these women. Respondents also reported considerable worry over health and income adequacy.

868. Kivett, Vira R., and Jean P. Scott. "Rural Frail Older Women: Implications for Policy and Planning." _Journal of Minority Aging_, 4:113-122 (1979).

> An analysis of data collected in Kivett's study from 418 rural North Carolina elderly. The focus here is on the general characteristics of 82 females aged 75-99. Reports data on basic socio-demographic indicators, health, familial network, and problems.

869. Lenihan, Ayeliffe Arline Hildegarde. "A profile of rural elderly women: an assessment of human functioning and available resources." (Doctoral dissertation, University of Maryland, College Park, Maryland, 1979.) _Dissertation Abstracts International_, 40, 5, A, p.3585.

> Presents findings on the general well being of a sample of elderly females living in six rural areas. The respondents were found to have good social resources but be mildly impaired in terms of economic resources, physical health, and mental health.

870. Sebastian, Margaret. See entry number 11.

871. Stojanovic, Elisabeth J. See entry number 403.

872. United States Senate, Special Committee on Aging. Impact of federal estate tax policies on rural women. (Hearing, 97th Congress, 1st Session, February 4th.) Washington, D. C.: United States Government Printing Office, 1981.

Contains articles, statements, correspondence.

873. Wilkinson, Carroll Wetzel. See entry number 179.

874. Youmans, E. Grant. See entry number 798.

AUTHOR INDEX

GEOGRAPHIC INDEX

....

About the Compiler

JOHN A. KROUT is Associate Professor of Sociology at the State University of New York at Fredonia where he is also Director of Sponsored Research. He has contributed articles to journals including *The Gerontologist, Rural Sociology,* and *Research on Aging,* and has presented numerous papers on the rural elderly at professional conferences. Professor Krout's research is funded by the Administration on Aging and the American Association of Retired Persons (AARP) Andrus Foundation.

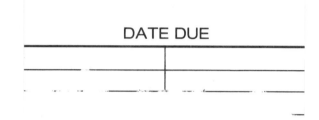